# THE WISDOM OF
# ISRAEL REGARDIE

෴ ෴ ෴ ෴ ෴

VOLUME II
SELECTED ESSAYS
AND COMMENTARIES

# Some Other Titles From New Falcon Publications

| | |
|---|---|
| Aha! The Sevenfold Mystery of the Ineffable Love | Aleister Crowley |
| Bio-Etheric Healing | Trudy Lanitis |
| Undoing Yourself With Energized Meditation and Other Devices | |
| Secrets of Western Tantra: The Sexuality of the Middle Path | |
| Dogma Daze | Christopher S. Hyatt, Ph.D. |
| Rebels & Devils; The Psychology of Liberation | Edited by Christopher S. Hyatt, Ph.D. |
| Aleister Crowley's Illustrated Goetia | |
| Taboo: Sex, Religion & Magick | |
| Sex Magic, Tantra & Tarot: The Way of the Secret Lover | |
| | Christopher S. Hyatt, Ph.D., and Lon Milo DuQuette |
| Pacts With The Devil | |
| Urban Voodoo: A Beginner's Guide to Afro-Caribbean Magic | |
| | Jason Black and Christopher S. Hyatt, Ph.D. |
| The Psychopath's Bible | Christopher S. Hyatt, Ph.D., and Jack Willis |
| Ask Baba Lon | Lon Milo DuQuette |
| Aleister Crowley and the Treasure House of Images | J.F.C. Fuller, Aleister Crowley, Lon Milo DuQuette and Nancy Wasserman |
| Enochian World of Aleister Crowley | Lon Milo DuQuette and Aleister Crowley |
| Info-Psychology   Neuropolitique   The Game of Life | |
| What Does WoMan Want? | Timothy Leary, Ph.D. |
| Be Yourself - A Guide to Relaxation and Health | |
| Dr. Israel Regardie's Definitive Work on Aleister Crowley, The Eye In The Triangle | |
| Healing Energy, Prayer and Relaxation | |
| My Rosicrucian Adventure | |
| Teachers of Fulfillment | |
| The Complete Golden Dawn System of Magic | |
| The Eye in the Triangle: An Interpretation of Aleister Crowley | |
| The Golden Dawn Audio CDs | |
| The Legend of Aleister Crowley | |
| The Portable Complete Golden Dawn System of Magic | |
| The Tree of Life | |
| What You Should Know About the Golden Dawn | Dr. Israel Regardie |
| Roll Away The Stone/The Herb Dangerous | Dr. Israel Regardie and Aleister Crowley |
| Rebellion, Revolution and Religiousness | Osho |
| Reichian Therapy: A Practical Guide for Home Use | Dr. Jack Willis |
| Woman's Orgasm: A Guide to Sexual Satisfaction | Benjamin Graber, M.D., and Georgia Kline-Graber, R.N. |
| Shaping Formless Fire   Seizing Power   Taking Power | Stephen Mace |
| The Illuminati Conspiracy: The Sapiens System | Donald Holmes, M.D. |
| The Secret Inner Order Rituals of the Golden Dawn | Pat Zalewski |
| Sufism, Islam and Jungian Psychology | J. Marvin Spiegelman, Ph.D. |
| Nonlocal Nature: The Eight Circuits of Consciousness | James A. Heffernan |
| on What is | Ja Wallin |

**MANY OF OUR TITLES AVAILABLE ON KINDLE!**
Please visit our website at http://www.newfalcon.com

# THE WISDOM OF
# ISRAEL REGARDIE

༄ ༄ ༄ ༄ ༄

## VOLUME II
### SELECTED ESSAYS AND COMMENTARIES

NEW FALCON PUBLICATIONS
LAS VEGAS, NEVADA, U.S.A.

Copyright © 2018 New Falcon Publications

All rights reserved. No part of this book,
in part or in whole, may be reproduced, transmitted,
or utilized, in any form or by any means, electronic or mechanical,
including photocopying, recording, or by any information storage
and retrieval system, without permission in writing
from the publisher, except for brief quotations
in critical articles, books and reviews.

ISBN 13: 978-1-56184-548-4
ISBN 10: 1-56184-548-5

New Falcon Publications First Edition

The paper used in this publication meets the minimum requirements
of the American National Standard for Permanence of
Paper for Printed Library Materials Z39.48-1984

Printed in USA

NEW FALCON PUBLICATIONS
9550 South Eastern Avenue • Suite 253
Las Vegas, NV 89123
www.newfalcon.com
email: info@newfalcon.com

# Introduction

## By James Wasserman

Israel Regardie (1907–1985) was a one-of-kind phenomena. He can be described as a pioneer in several fields, a polymath who explored and contributed to the modern spiritual path in several unique ways. Regardie was a true trailblazer.

Born in London, his family moved to America in 1921, and he attended art school in Philadelphia. He began his esoteric studies at age fifteen reading Madame Blavatsky. This was a remarkably young age at this period of history, pre-Internet, and well before the popularization of Occult and New Age studies. He continued with his teenage studies to an exploration of yoga and Hindu philosophy and religion, and, later, Buddhism.

At the age of eighteen, Regardie came in contact with Crowley's *Book Four: Part One, Meditation*. This book is a brilliant and rational exploration of yoga and Eastern philosophy. It completely dispenses with the exaggerated religiosity of classic Hindu methodology, and the entire range of accretions of superstition and culturally-specific maxims so common to most all of the other writers of the day. Crowley offered a common sense, scientific appraisal of the topic, as well as the viewpoint of an educated practitioner who had mastered so many of the practices about which he wrote. Regardie was astounded.

He then wrote to Karl Germer, Crowley's American representative and, later, successor. The two met and Regardie purchased a set of *The Equinox* along with several other Crowley books.

He immersed himself in these works, a curriculum of attainment with a literal treasure trove of theory, practices, philosophy, and reading lists of suggested additional materials. Regardie was hooked. In my experience, it is very difficult for a Western person to integrate the cultural concepts so often found in Eastern spiritual literature. Crowley refined the essentials of all these teachings to a palatable, rational, and comprehensible language that leaves a Western student in familiar territory. The intellect is not insulted by being trivialized. The references are those to the society in which we live. Crowley was speaking and Regardie was listening.

Germer passed along Regardie's name to Crowley with what one can only assume was an enthusiastic character reference. Crowley and Regardie then began their own correspondence. In 1928, the 21-year-old Regardie set sail for Europe to begin his employment as Aleister Crowley's personal secretary. Thus began what would be the central relationship of Regardie's life.

He discusses much of this in his excellent biography of Crowley, *The Eye in the Triangle*, published by New Falcon Publications. This was also a memoir of Regardie's personal experiences with Crowley, cataloging much personal suffering and development, as the young man became deeply schooled in the ways of the world by his teacher. A series of financial difficulties led to Crowley being unable to continue employing his secretary and Regardie set off in 1931 to greener pastures. Their parting was amicable.

Regardie soon went on to write *The Garden of Pomegranates* and *The Tree of Life*, the first on Qabalah and the second on Magick and Crowley's system. Both are dedicated to Crowley (and both also published by New Falcon Publications). Several years later, around 1937, their friendship would end as Crowley mocked Regardie and the latter fired back with both barrels.

Despite the problems between them, Regardie would be greatly responsible for the blossoming of Crowley's works in the early

1970s. His *Eye in the Triangle* was the first coherent biography of Crowley written by an actual student and practitioner of Magick. His *Tree of Life* (reprinted in 1969) is an important and serious study of Crowley's work which became widely available throughout the U.S. and England during the Occult Revival of this period.

After leaving Crowley's employ, Regardie joined the Stella Matutina in 1934, after publishing his two books and meeting Dion Fortune. This would become another key developmental stage in his life, as he embraced the magical and qabalistic spiritual teachings of this order, including its Christian basis. The Stella Matutina was a later development of the crucial Hermetic Order of the Golden Dawn—where Crowley had received his initial training and which served as the creative model for so many magical groups to come. Crowley and Regardie both loved the brilliant weave of information and elegant symbolism within the order, derived primarily from the minds of two qabalistic scholars: S. L. MacGregor Mathers and W. Wynn Westcott.

As Crowley had done in The Equinox in 1909 and 1910, Regardie published many of the secrets of the Golden Dawn from 1938 to 1940 in his own four-volume *Golden Dawn*. It has since been republished and updated as *The Complete Golden Dawn System of Magic* by New Falcon. Regardie's work provided the essential materials for the resurrection of the Golden Dawn worldwide, and all the activities which have taken place since.

Regardie was also one of the first Westerners to insist on the relationship between health and the spiritual life. In his *Be Yourself*, and *The Art of True Healing* (both now published by New Falcon), he advanced the notion that proper spiritual health demands that the initiate respect the physical body as a vehicle of incarnation. This has given rise to the modern science and art of holistic health, and the fascination with proper diet and living. Regardie was a licensed and practicing chiropractor.

Regardie was also the first magician to popularize the connection between psychotherapy and Magick. As anyone with any experience in the field is only too well aware, Magick attracts neurotics and fantasists of all stripes. It can also reveal long-buried neurosis in even the most stable practitioner. Accepting this reality, Regardie echoed the ancient teachings of the Mysteries of Eleusis, "Know Thyself." He was a particularly fervent proponent of the work of Wilhelm Reich, which is concerned with the energy blockages resulting from psychological maladjustment and trauma. Reich could be called the magician's psychotherapist. Regardie insisted on psychotherapy as a preliminary part of the magician's path.

This collection of Regardie's writings offers much insight into his varied interests, along with much practical information for the esoteric student. Combining magical practices with spiritual commentary, psychological insights with alchemy, Tarot and occult history, Regardie's wide erudition is well demonstrated. Whether one approaches these writings as a student of the Mysteries, a practical theorist of human behavior, a working alchemist, one interested in the interaction between psychology, culture, and politics, or a combination of all of the above, the wit, wisdom, and guidance offered here by Dr. Regardie will prove invaluable. Thanks to New Falcon for assembling this multifaceted group of essays.

Regardie's personal life served as a perfect example of the values we seek in an initiate. He was filled with a great sense of humor, and an infectious charisma, combined with the indefatigable energy of a truly well-balanced and healthy individual. His rigorous integrity demanded that he change his views of Crowley despite the pain that Crowley had caused him in his youth. He, perhaps reluctantly at first, became one of Crowley's greatest defenders in a time when this was not a popular public position to take. Israel Regardie was a modern Giant.

# Table of Contents

| | |
|---|---|
| Introduction by *James Wasserman* | v |
| Commentary by Israel Regardie on Aleister Crowley's *AHA! The Sevenfold Mystery of the Ineffable Love* | 3 |
| *Pentagram Rituals from The Complete Golden Dawn System of Magic* | 21 |
| *London Forum 1933, New Messiahs Letter to Editor* | 37 |
| *What is Psychotherapy?* | 41 |
| *Cry Havoc* | 57 |
| *On Reich* | 69 |
| *Aspiration and the "Mother Complex"* | 79 |
| *Alchemy in the World Today* | 107 |
| Introduction to *The Complete Golden Dawn System of Magic* | 115 |
| *The 78 Tarot Cards* from the *The Complete Golden Dawn System of Magic* | 137 |
| *The Fellowship of the Rosey Cross* | 179 |

# ESSAYS AND COMMENTARIES
## by Israel Regardie

# AHA!
## The Sevenfold Mystery of the Ineffable Love
By Aleister Crowley
A Commentary by Israel Regardie
New Falcon Publications, 1983

To have chosen so unlikely a title as *AHA!* for an almost epic poem about mysticism must require a strangely constituted mind. And this, of course, is supremely applicable to Aleister Crowley, an English poet born in Leamington in the year 1875. As a result of many years of concentrated study of comparative religions, mythology, mysticism of every variety and magical practices picked up in remote parts of the world, his mind had developed into a highly intricate mnemonic apparatus. One word or phrase would immediately serve as a trigger to set into operation a long chain of associations trailing obscurely into a lifelong collection of fascinating ideas. For the most part they would stagger any newcomer to his innumerable writings.

The word *AHA!* had come to have innumerable meanings for Crowley. Some were derived from the Qabalah which he had studied through the Hermetic Order of the Golden Dawn. It has a gematria or numerical value of seven, relates to the sphere of Venus on the Tree of Life, and the element Fire. In one Tarot document of the Order, the sevens are described as showing "a force, transcending the material plane, and is like unto a crown which is indeed powerful but requireth one capable of wearing it."

Other associations had their origins in the Bible, of which he had long been a close student–especially the Revelation of St. John. This is indicated, for example, in the subtitle which Crowley chose for this poem, part of which is as follows: The Sevenfold Mystery of the Ineffable Love: the Coming of the Lord in the Air as King and Judge of this corrupted World..." The major pitfall where he became trapped was in the assumption that the ordinary reader's mind would be equally informed as was his, or that it would function similarly to his. Of course this was hardly the case.

The historical sequence of events leading up to the creation of *AHA!* is fascinating. In 1887, and English Occult society known as The Golden Dawn was founded by Dr. William Westcott, MacGregor Mathers and Dr. W. R. Woodman as an outgrowth of some earlier Masonic organizations. Through correspondence with a woman known as Fräulein Anna Sprengel (Soror S.D.A.), they made contact with European secret societies having possible Rosicrucian connections. Since that time, the Order has exerted a greater influence on the growth and dissemination of occultism than most students realize. Its membership was recruited from every circle, and included physicians, clergymen, artists and humble men and women from all walks of life. It is now common knowledge that S. L. MacGregor Mathers, A. E. Waite, Florence Farr and Dion Fortune were members, together with a good many other writers and artists.

As an organization, it preferred always to shroud itself in an impenetrable cloak of mystery. Its teaching and methods of instruction were stringently guarded by various penalties attached to the most awe-inspiring obligations in order to ensure secrecy. So well were these obligations respected, with but a couple of exceptions, that for years the general public knew next to nothing about the Order and what it stood for.

Crowley was initiated into this Order on November 18, 1898. He made rapid strides in advancement. But the really significant event during his membership was meeting one of its advanced adept members named Allan Bennett. He understood the intricacies of Qabalah and Magic on all levels. Allan was a good teacher, for the traces of his instruction appear in almost everything that Crowley wrote.

A revolt broke out within the Order, splitting it wide open. Allan Bennett went to the East, adopting the Buddhist faith with the new name of Bhikhu Ananda Metteya. Crowley left England to go mountain-climbing in Mexico with Oscar Eckenstein, a famous mountain-climber of that period. They planned an assault on one of the lofty peaks of the Himalayas. Eckenstein was to return to England to make all arrangements for the climb, since he was to be in charge of the expedition.

Crowley, on his way to the Himalayas, stopped off first in Ceylon, ostensibly to meet once more his former teacher, Allan Bennett. However, while in Ceylon, they both settled down to an intense practice of Yoga under the supervision of Shri Parananda, the former Solicitor General of Ceylon. This bout of Yoga practice culminated for Crowley in an illumination known as Dhyana.

When he came to write *AHA!* this Dhyana was described as some length. A part of that writing is:

...Again,
The adept secures his subtle fence
Against the hostile shafts of sense,
Pins for a second his mind; as you
May have seen some huge wrestler do.
With all his gathered weight heaped, hurled,
Resistless as the whirling world,
He holds his foeman to the floor
For one great moment and no more.
So–then the sun-blaze! All the night
Bursts to a vivid orb of light.
There is no shadow; nothing is,
But the intensity of bliss.
Being is blasted. That exists.

This man Crowley is such a paradox. One would have thought that having reached this stage of enlightenment, he would have persevered further. On the contrary, he discarded all yoga practices, resumed mountain climbing, failed in the assault against a high Himalayan peak and returned to Scotland rather disgusted and dejected.

An artist friend of his, Gerald Kelly–who later became President of the Royal Academy–arranged to introduce Crowley to his sister Rose. She was about to get married to a man for whom she cared little. While discouraging her to proceed with this marriage, Crowley impulsively proposed to her–and forthwith they eloped.

Married life was a deliriously happy period of exultant eroticism, wide travelling and a variety of expeditions and hunting trips with his wife. Early in the year 1904, during a safari in Ceylon, Rose became pregnant. At once Crowley called off the hunt and decided to return to Scotland, stopping off on the way in Cairo, mostly to avoid the inclement weather of the British Isles. By this time, according to his own account, he had renounced all of his earlier interests in magic and yoga, living, for the moment, the life of an ordinary English family man.

However, despite his disavowal of occultism, during their stay in Cairo a most remarkable series of events occurred. Crowley had been performing a ritual with the intention of showing his wife the sylphs, or air spirits. Rose, who was a devoted and superficial socialite when Crowley first met her, spontaneously developed a psychic or mediumistic talent. Although she did not see the sylphs, she entered a peculiar, dreamy state of mind and told Crowley that "they are waiting for you." He was then enamored of his wife, but he had very little respect for her intellectual abilities or her psychic gifts. He was also a confirmed skeptic and free-thinker, so he subjected her to a battery of tests based on his own knowledge and former magical experience.

The full account of this altogether remarkable episode has been narrated in full in Crowley's book *The Equinox of the Gods*. I have also discussed this in my biographical study of him entitled *The Eye in the Triangle* (New Falcon Publications). A long story is unnecessary here. Suffice it to say that every day for three days he was instructed to sit alone in the living room of their Cairo apartment. For one full hour on each of three successive days beginning on April 8th, a voice dictated to him what was called *The Book of Law*, sometimes written as *Liber AL vel Legis*.

This document enunciated a series of new moral, religious, mystical and philosophical dogmas. Some of these he was already familiar with and could accept without equivocation. Many passages dealt with the teachings of the Golden Dawn whose rituals were announced as abrogate and out of touch with the dawning new age. Others were so revolutionary and distasteful to him that he responded to his extraordinary psychic experience with a classic Freudian psychological mechanism. He buried the holograph manuscript amongst a host of miscellaneous materials stored in the attic of his house at Boleskine, Scotland, and then promptly forgot all about it.

It is still unclear why he really rejected *The Book of Law*. After all, it did praise him to the skies. It called him a prophet who was a revealer of a New Aeon dawning for mankind–and it declared and hymned his unique status, "and blessing & worship to the prophet of the lovely Star." A modest man might easily have been offended by this unequivocal aggrandizement of the ego. But Crowley was under no circumstances a modest, retiring sort of creature–despite the fact that he realized the fallacies of an ego-oriented philosophy as *AHA!* clearly shows.

> Cease to strive!
> Destroy this partial I, this moan
> Of an hurt beast!...
>
> Indeed, that "I" that is not God
> Is but a lion in the road!

In spite of this, he withdrew from the world-shaking role depicted for him in *The Book of Law*; he would not accept it.

For five years he went about his business–being a husband and father, a writer of many poetic works, a mountain climber of a second Himalayan expedition, etc.–as if he had never been the recipient of a new revelation. But the praeter-human agencies behind the dictation of this magical document slowly wore down his stubborn resistance. One seemingly accidental phenomenon after another occurred with dreadful frequency until at last he became willing to assume the mantle of prophet that had been cast upon him.

One day, while hunting on behalf of a friend for a pair of skis in the attic of his house in Scotland, he suddenly fell upon the manuscript of *The Book of Law*. He was overwhelmed. It was as if this unwanted discovery in the year 1909 were the last straw. In a spontaneous act of wonder as well as submission, he fell in line. He accepted the responsibilities that were spelled out in detail in *The Book of Law*. One of the several results ensuing from this conversion-like acceptance was the writing of *AHA!*

In this lengthy poem, he attempts to tie together a number of loose threads in his life, as well as to affirm the supreme fact that he was a messenger bearing a message. *AHA!* may be considered the poetic clarification of what he finally stood for.

The poem describes in great fullness, and with extraordinary power and eloquence, the mystical path in all its varieties that he was familiar with from a practical and experimental point of view. The eight limbs of Yoga are described in a long paragraph, which incidentally has been used by many writers without the least bit of acknowledgment. This paragraph begins:

> There are seven keys to the great gate,
> Being eight in one and one in eight...

And ends with:

> ...I leave thee here:
> Thou art the Master. I revere
> Thy radiance that rolls afar
> O Brother of the Silver Star!

This is followed by some descriptions of the early phases of magical practice, particularly that called in the Golden Dawn "skrying in the spirit vision," which, pursued properly to it's logical end, may lead to higher mystical states:

> The first true sights. Bright images
> Throng the clear mind at first, a crowd
> Of Gods, lights, armies, landscapes; loud
> Reverberations of the Light.
> But these are dreams, things in the mind,
> Reveries, idols. Thou shalt find
> No rest therein. The former three
> (Lightning, moon, sun) are royally
> Liminal to the Hall of Truth.
> Also here be with them in sooth,
> Their brethren. There's the vision called
> The Lion of the Light, a brand
> Of ruby flame and emerald
> Waved by the Hermeneutic Hand.
> There is the Chalice, whence the flood
> of God's beatitude of blood
> Flames. O to sing those starry tunes!
> O colder than a million moons!
> O vestal waters! Wine of love
> Wan as the lyric soul thereof!
> There is the Wind, a whirling sword,
> The savage rapture of the air
> Tossed beyond space and time. My Lord,
> My Lord, even now I see Thee there

In infinite motion! And beyond
There is the Disk, the wheel of things;
Like a black boundless diamond
Whirring with millions of wings!

This poem contains other descriptions of mystical states, unique in the annals of religious literature. I have in mind particularly that account of a shattering experience which I believe occurred in 1906 or 1907 during or shortly after Crowley's walk through the southern part of China near the present Vietnam border. This account bears comparison with that of Sir Edwin Arnold's translation of *The Bhagavad Gita* which is called *The Song Celestial*. In that comparison, it may be said that Crowley's account does not come off a poor second.

OLYMPAS: Tell me thereof!
MARSYAS: Oh not of this!
Of all the flowers in God's field
We name not this. Our lips are sealed
In that the Universal Key
Lieth within its mystery.
But know thou this. These visions give
A hint both faint and fugitive
Yet haunting, that behind them lurks
Some Worker, greater that His works.
[...]
The infinite Lord of Light and Love
Breaks on the soul like dawn. See! See!
Great God of Might and Majesty!
Beyond sense, beyond sight, a brilliance
Burning from His glowing glance!
Formless, all the worlds of flame
Atoms of that fiery frame!

> The adept caught up and broken;
> Slain, before His Name be spoken!
> In that fire the soul burns up.
> One drop from that celestial cup
> Is an abyss, an infinite sea
> That sucks up immortality!
> O but the Self is manifest
> Through all that blaze! Memory stumbles
> Like a blind man for all the rest.
> Speech, like a crag of limestone, crumbles,
> While this one soul of thought is sure
> Through all the confusion to endure,
> Infinite Truth in one small span:
> This that is God is Man.

There is also an account, brief to be sure, but hauntingly beautiful of the so-called Abra-Melin Operation. This celebrated magical retirement has its original description in The Book of the *Sacred Magic of Abra-Melin the Mage*, translated from the French many decades ago by MacGregor Mathers.

The author of this book is supposed to have been one Abraham, named Abra-Melin. There is undoubtedly mythology here, but that is altogether unimportant. Regardless of its origin, its date and its authorship, this work was found to be of value to some of the adepts of the Golden Dawn and many other students. The author makes no impossible demands such as are found in the fraudulent grimoires concerning the blood of bats caught at midnight, or the fourth feather from the left wing of a completely black cock, or the stuffed eye of a virgin basilisk, and so on.

Though perhaps some of the requirements are difficult to follow, there is always an excellent reason for their inclusion.

They are not intended to be subtle tests of the skill of the operator. Certain preliminary prescriptions and injunctions need to be observed, but these really amount to little more than common-sense counsel, to observe decency in the performance of so august an operation.

For example, one should possess a house where proper precautions against disturbance and interference can be taken. This having been arranged, there remains but little else to do. For six months in privacy, the sole preoccupation is to aspire with increasing concentration and ardor towards the Knowledge and Conversation of the Holy Guardian Angel.

It was in the year 1899 that Crowley originally began this particular retirement. However, shortly after he started, the revolt broke out in earnest among the members of the Golden Dawn. Upon hearing of this, Crowley immediately terminated the Operation and wired MacGregor Mathers, offering his services and his fortune should they be needed. Crowley found himself in the midst of a hornet's nest, and was blamed for a great deal for which he had no responsibility at all.

After his 1902 Himalayan debacle, he returned to England somewhat dejected and dismayed. He met Rose Kelly and married her on the spur of the moment. But it had been his intention to start the Operation a second time. During the previous three or four years, he had gained enough experience with magic and yoga to realize that his first attempt would have resulted in failure because of a lack of proper preparation. His current preoccupation with his new wife was so complete however, that naturally there was neither time nor interest in anything else, including Abra-Melin.

His next serious attempt was made during the walk across the southern boundaries of China in 1906. He was accompanied by his wife and child and a faithful servant. There were times when one or the other was ill, or some unforeseen but serious danger threatened. Yet throughout a period of several months, perched on a small pony, this strange and intrepid aspirant to adeptship was performing a complex magical ceremony with ardor and enthusiasm. In a Temple not built with hands, he had constructed the Abramelin environment astrally in his trained imagination, to follow the lines of instruction he had previously received while a member of the Order.

> And at the midnight thou shalt go
> To the mid-stream's smoothest flow,
> And strike upon a golden bell
> The spirit's call; then say the spell:
> "Angel, mine angel, draw thee nigh!"
> Making the Sign of Magistry
> With wand of lapis lazuli.
> Then, it may be, through the blind dumb
> Night thou shalt see thine angel come,
> [...]
> He shall inform his happy lover;
> My foolish prating shall be over!

Foolish prating or not, the poem continues this early theme with that which results from sincere and patient discipline.

> Angel, I invoke thee now!
> Bend on me the starry brow!
> Spread the eagle wings above
> The pavilion of our love!...

[...]
O thou art like a Hawk of Gold,
Miraculously manifold,
For all the sky's aflame to be
A mirror magical of Thee!
The stars seem comets, rushing down
To gem thy robes, bedew thy crown
Like the moon-plumes of a strange bird
By a great wind sublimely stirred,
Thou drawest the light of all the skies
Into thy wake. The heaven dies
In bubbling froth of light, that foams
About thine ardour. All the domes
Of all the heavens close above thee.
Excellent kiss, though fastenest on
This soul of mine, that it is gone,
Gone from all life, and rapt away
Into the infinite starry spray
Of thine own Æon...Alas for me!
I faint. Thy mystic majesty
Absorbs this spark.

Some of the lovely phrases and sentences in these quotations from AHA! have been with me for many long years.

Lie open, a chameleon cup,
And let Him suck thine honey up!!

And again,

Angel, mine Angel, draw Thee nigh!

These phrases, with another from an earlier mystical prose-poem entitled *Liber VII vel Lapidis Lazuli*, were responsible forty years ago for one of the premonitory religious or mystical experiences of my burgeoning spiritual life.

There are dozens more. The aspirant who has been duly prepared by life, experience and study will find his own cues to serve as catalysts of the inner life. Each reader is bound to discover his own individual set of stimuli. They are there for the finding.

Another experience of major spiritual significance followed within months of Crowley's rediscovery of the manuscript of *The Book of Law* and his acceptance of his destiny as therein described. He undertook a trip to the Sahara Desert in 1909 with his discipline, Victor B. Neuburg. During their walk, Crowley would invoke every day, one of the Aethyrs of the Enochian system of magic. Neuburg would act as the scribe for Crowley's visions. The complex Enochian magical system had been developed in the late 1500s by Queen Elizabeth's astrologer Dr. John Dee working in collaboration with a notorious alchemist, Sir Edward Kelly. The Golden Dawn later transformed their skeletal records into a superb system which synthesized every single component of its teaching.

After invoking the Angel of each successive Aethyr, Crowley would enter a semi-trance, dictating what he heard and saw to Neuburg, who would record it all. This record later became *The Vision and the Voice*, a most remarkable spiritual document. It is important to mention it here because in the course of these daily invocations and apocalyptic visions, *The Book of the Law* was referred to again to again. The visions confirmed Crowley's act of submission, and directed his attention to the task confronting him.

The desert experience resulted in Crowley's second crossing of the Abyss, a critical event in his spiritual life. It was then that he chose the magical motto of *Vi Veri Universum Vivus Vici*, or V.V.V.V.V.

This crossing of the Abyss is not the "sweet and light" phenomenon many amateur mystics would have us believe. Even Dr. Carl G. Jung asserts that coming to know God may be fraught with horror and terror before man will let go of his ego. It is generally accompanied by a "coming apart at the seams" of the mind.

All mystics of every age have described in various ways this major disintegration, purgation or submission of the soul, prior to its confrontation with God, in acquisition of cosmic consciousness. Nowhere is it described so eloquently as the species of insanity that it is as in our present poem.

> Black snare that I was taken in!
> How one may pass I hardly know.
> Maybe Time never blots the track.
> Black, black, intolerably black!
> Go, spectre of the ages, go!
> Suffice it that I passed beyond.
> I found the secret of the bond
> Of thought to thought through countless years,
> Through many lives, in many spheres,
> Brought to a point the dark design
> Of this existence that is mine. *All I was*
> I brought into the burning-glass
> And all its focused light and heat
> Charred *all I am*. The rune's complete
> When *all I shall be* flashes by
> Like a shadow on the sky.
> Then I dropped my reasoning.
> Vacant and accursed thing!....

It is only after the delineation of this crossing that Crowley proceeds to instruction in basic techniques, and finally to expound the Law as laid down in *Liber Legis*.

> Do what thou wilt! is the sole word
> Of Law that my attainment heard.

Here is given the central core of the 1904 revelation to which he devoted, in one way or another, the remaining years of his life.

> Arise, and set a period
> Unto Restriction! That is sin:
> To hold thine holy spirit in!

The rest of the epic deals with transcriptions and descriptions of the parts of the three chapters of that devastating Book.

The format of the poem consists of a dialogue between a teacher Marsysas and his pupil, Olympas. Crowley provides a brief description of his intent in a preliminary survey of the poem called "The Argumentation." He opens this by stating:

> A little before Dawn, the pupil comes to greet his Master, and begs instruction."

In passing, I ought to make note that in 1932, when I wrote *The Tree of Life* (Samuel Weiser, Inc.)–which expressed my comprehension of Crowley's magic up to that time–the dedication was: "To Marsyas, with poignant memory of what might have been." In the course of the past three or four decades, I have met no one who had the least inkling of the meaning of the dedication, which simply means that this lovely poetic saga of Crowley's own odyssey, to be found in *The Equinox*, I, 3, was known to pitifully few people. Actually it expressed sadness and regret on my part that Crowley had not strictly attended to the magical training that was promised me in 1928 when I had joined him in Paris. An easing of that disappointment came later, when I realized that he was temporarily in a state of what could be called spiritual paralysis and some psycho-social disorganization resulting from the stresses and strains of the previous years.

Let me close by saying that the main body of *AHA!* is superb. It includes some powerful and magnificent poetry which needs to be preserved for posterity–to whom, I hope, it will be as meaningful and inspirational as it has been to me.

August 22, 1969
Studio City, California

## *THE PENTAGRAM RITUALS*
### *from The Complete Golden Dawn System of Magic*
By Israel Regardie
New Falcon Publications, First Edition 1984

## THE PENTAGRAM
## RITUAL OF AIR

1. Perform the Lesser Banishing Ritual of the Pentagram.

2. Perform the Lesser Invoking Ritual of the Air Pentagram.

3. Face East. Feel breezes coming eastward or from the East, and feel that the breeze goes right through you, coming into the front and going out the back. After having got the wind through, try to feel the wind as yellow. See a stream of yellow light emanating from this particular cardinal point.

4. Vibrate each of the following Names as often as you feel inclined:

SHADDAI EL CHAI (Divine Name)
RAPHEL (Archangelic Name)
CHASSAN (Angelic Name)

5. Visualize Sylphs–little fairy-like figures. Let your imagination run away with you as with the Gnomes, but do not force

it. Remember they are trying to subtilize, trying to eliminate the gross, and trying to make everything in which the Light can function. Let the cramp of the mind go and let the mind play with these fairy-like Sylphs. Feel that they are pouring through you.

6. Recite the Invocation. It is the Prayer of the Sylphs. REMEMBER YOUR IDEA OF GRATITUDE. You, too, must help, even as they are helping you. They have no consciousness in our sense of the work. Having no consciousness, they have no sense of a goal, and we must give them a concept of goal. And for the benefit of all the Sylphs in our Nature, we recite the Invocation and we inspire them to our goal.

Holy art thou, Lord of the Air,
Who has created the Firmament.
SHADDAI EL CHAI.
Almighty and everlasting,
Ever-magnified in the life of all.
We praise Thee, and we bless Thee,
In the changeless empire of created Light;
And we aspire without cessation unto thine
Imperishable and Immutable Brilliance. AMEN

7. Perform Banishing Ritual.

8. Perform meditation.

## THE PENTAGRAM
## RITUAL OF FIRE

1. Perform the Lesser Banishing Ritual of the Pentagram.

2. Perform the Lesser Invoking Ritual of the Fire Pentagram.

3. Face South.

4. Vibrate each of the following Names as often as you feel inclined:

YHVH TZABAOTH (Divine Name)
MICHEL (Archangelic Name)
ARAL (Angelic Name)

As you vibrate the Names, imagine a flame as coming into the room from the South, either as flame or as definite entities. See yourself as being licked by the flame, scorched by them, and see the elementals working upon you in the same way as the Gnomes, Sylphs, and Undines.

5. Visualize Salamanders.

6. Recite the Invocation. It is the Prayer of the Salamanders. REMEMBER YOUR IDEA OF GRATITUDE. You, too, must help them, even as they are helping you. They have no consciousness in our sense of the work. Having no consciousness, they have no sense of goal, and we must give them a concept of goal. And for the benefit of all the Salamanders in our Nature, we recite the Invocation and we inspire them to our goal.

Holy art Thou, Lord of the Fire,
Wherein Thou has shown forth
The Throne of thy Glory.
YOD-HEH-VAV-HEH TZABAOTH.
Leader of Armies is thy Holy Name.
O Thou flashing Fire,
Thou illuminest all things
With thine insupportable Refulgence
Whence flow the ceaseless streams of Splendour
Which nourisheth thine Infinite Spirit.
Help us, thy children, whom Thou hast loved
Since the birth of the Ages of Time. AMEN.

7. Perform Banishing Ritual.

8. Perform meditation.

## THE PENTAGRAM RITUAL OF WATER

1. Perform the Lesser Banishing Ritual of the Pentagram.

2. Perform the Lesser Invoking Ritual of the Water Pentagram.

3. Face West. There must be relaxation of mind, relaxed enough to let the subtle currents flow through from the Undines in whom the force comes up. We assist the Undines by our Prayer for the elemental. We enable them to formulate in consciousness for what they unconsciously feel.

4. Vibrate each of the following Names as often as you feel inclined:

ELOHIM TZABAOTH (Divine Name)
GABRIEL (Archangelic Name)
TALIHAD (Angelic Name)

5. Visualize Undines.

6. Recite the Invocation. It is the Prayer of the Undines. REMEMBER YOUR IDEA OF GRATITUDE. You, too, must help them, even as they are helping you. They have no consciousness in our sense of the work. Having no consciousness, they have no sense of a goal, and we must give them a concept of goal. And for the benefit of all the Undines in our Nature, we recite the Invocation and we inspire them to our goal.

Holy art Thou, Lord of the Mighty Waters,
Whereon Thy spirit moved in the Beginning.

ELOHIM TZABAOTH.
Glory be unto Thee RUACH ELOHIM,
Whose Spirit hovered over the
Great Waters of Creation.
O Depth, O inscrutable Depth,
Which exhalest unto the height;
Lead Thou us into the true Life.
Through sacrifice, through Love,
So that one day we may be found
Worthy to offer unto Thee,
The Water, the Blood and the Tears,
For the remission of sins. AMEN.

7. Perform Banishing Ritual.

8. Perform meditation.

## THE PENTAGRAM
## RITUAL OF EARTH

1. Perform the Lesser Banishing Ritual of the Pentagram.

2. Perform the Lesser Invoking Ritual of the Earth Pentagram.

3. Face North, Visualize lying on cool, black, rich earth. Visualize earth all around you, and penetrating right through your open pores to the center of your being.

4. Vibrate each of the following Names as often as you feel inclined:

ADONAI HA-ARETZ (Divine Name)
AURIEL (Archangelic Name)
PHORLAKH (Angelic Name)

5. Visualize Gnomes–on the earth, under the earth, on your body, in your body–myriads of them, and let your imagination (without forcing) see these Gnomes playing, working, doing whatever comes into your mind. Especially watch their actions in your body.

6. Recite the Invocation. It is the Prayer of the Gnomes. REMEMBER YOUR IDEA OF GRATITUDE. You, too, must help them, even as they are helping you. They have no consciousness in our sense of the work. Having no consciousness, they have no sense of a goal, and we must give them a concept of goal. And for the benefit of all the Gnomes in our Nature, we recite the Invocation and we inspire them to our goal.

Holy, art Thou, Lord of the Earth,
Which Thou hast made for Thy footstool.
ADONAI HA-ARETZ, ADONAI MELEKH.
Unto Thee be the Kingdom, the Power, and the Glory.
MALKUTH-GEBURAH-GEDULAH, AMEN.

The Rose of Sharon, and the Lily of the Valley.
O Thou who hidest beneath the Earth,
In the Valley of Gems,
The marvelous seed of the Stars.
Live, reign, and be Thou the eternal
Dispenser of Thy treasures,
Whereof Thou hast made us
The wardens. AMEN.

7. Perform Banishing Ritual.

8. Perform meditation.

## THE PENTAGRAM
## RITUAL OF SPIRIT

We are dealing with a subject which is considerably more complex to discuss than any which we heretofore had. It is the Fifth Element–Ether or Akasha. The ancients did not include this as we have to look to the Alchemists for whatever we are able to give out regarding it. As soon as we reach this Fifth Element, we have difficulty in understanding what they meant. We have no prayer for the Fifth Element; but that there is a Fifth Element is fairly obvious. This Element is half manifest, half concealed. The Alchemists pay attention to five Elements and to the manipulating of this Fifth Element of Ether. The Fifth Element synthesizes the Four Elements and yet, although a synthesis is an Element by itself, this Fifth Element is a duality.

We will use the truncated pyramid. A truncated pyramid is one whose vertex is cut off by a plane usually parallel to the base. (The vertex of a pyramid is the point of intersection of the generating lines or boundary planes, respectively.) Each side of the truncated pyramid is considered to be one of the elements, Earth, Air, Fire, and Water. The base is OLAHM (the World). The top is ALEPH TAU–the Alpha and Omega, Spirit, and Essence–and it is directly involved here as the Fifth Element.

Imagine, after thoroughly relaxing, that you have built up a huge pyramid. See that Pyramid built up with all the imagination you have. You have to build up that Pyramid with the truncated top, and see yourself standing at the top. The East side of the Pyramid is Yellow in color, the South is Red, the West is Blue, and the North is Green. Expand your consciousness. Here, however, we approach a different concept, not Elemental, but Spiritual. Up to now we have dealt with the elemental side, the Green Ray. That was to strengthen the interior basis of your nature, so that now it will have something interior to work on. Enlarge your body to fill infinite Space so the forces of God can pour through you.

Inasmuch as there are some of you who are able to do this Ritual twice a day, I am going to give you variations of this in two ways because I do not want it mixed up with other work– not even in the Middle Pillar. Simply do this one thing. Of course you do the relaxation. It is always a part of your formula and routine.

1. Perform the Lesser Banishing Ritual of the Pentagram.

2. Perform the Greater Invoking Pentagram Ritual of Spirit, Active and Passive.

3. Face East and trace the Sign of Aquarius with your hand outstretched, and vibrate the appropriate divine Names I gave you for the Element of Air:

SHADDAI EL CHAI
RAPHEL
CHASSAN

Stand still and recite the prayer of Air, and at the same time imagine that the Sylphs are there and pouring through you:

Holy art Thou, Lord of the Air,
Who have created the Firmament.
SHADDAI EL CHAI.
Almighty and everlasting,
Ever-living be thy Name,
Ever-magnified in the life of all.
We praise Thee, and we bless Thee,

In the changeless empire of created Light;
And we aspire without cessation unto thine
Imperishable and Immutable Brilliance. AMEN.

4. Face South and trace the Sign of Leo. Then vibrate the appropriate divine Names of Fire:

YOD-HEH-VAV-HEH TZABAOTH
MICHEL
ARAL

Stand still and recite the prayer of Fire, and at the same time imagine that the Salamanders are there and pouring through you:

Holy art Thou, Lord of the Fire,
Wherein Thou hast shown forth
The Throne of thy Glory.
YOD-HEH-VAV-HEH TZABAOTH.
Leader of Armies is thy Holy Name.
O Thou flashing Fire,
Thou illuminest all things
With thine insupportable Refulgence
Whence flow the ceaseless streams of Splendour
Which nourisheth thine Infinite Spirit.
Help us, thy children, whom Thou hast loved
Since the birth of the Ages of Time. AMEN.

5. Face West and trace the Sign of Scorpio. Then vibrate the appropriate divine Names of Water:
ELOHIM TZABAOTH
GABRIEL
TALIHAD

Stand still and recite the prayer of Water, and at the same time imagine that the Undines are there and pouring through you:

Holy art Thou, Lord of the Mighty Waters,
Whereon Thy spirit moved in the Beginning.
ELOHIM TZABAOTH.
Glory be unto Thee RUACH ELOHIM,
Whose Spirit hovered over the
Great Waters of Creation.
O Depth, O inscrutable Depth,
Which exhalest unto the height;
Lead Thou us into the true Life,
Through sacrifice, through Love,
So that one day we may be found
Worthy to offer unto Thee,
The Water, the Blood and the Tears,
For the remission of sins. AMEN.

6. Face North and trace the Sign of Taurus. Then vibrate the appropriate divine Names of Earth:

ADONAI HA-ARETZ
AURIEL
PHORLAKI

Stand still and recite the prayer of Earth, and at the same time imagine that the Gnomes are there and pouring through you:

Holy art Thou, Lord of the Earth,
Which Thou hast made for Thy footstool.
ADONAI HA-ARETZ, ADONAI MELEKH.
Unto Thee be the Kingdom, the Power, and the Glory.

MALKUTH-GEBURAH-GEDULAH, AMEN.
The Rose of Sharon, and the Lily of the Valley.
O Thou who hidest beneath the Earth,
In the Valley of Gems,
The marvelous seed of the Stars.
Live, reign, and be Thou the eternal
Dispenser of Thy treasures,
Whereof Thou hast made us
The wardens. AMEN.

7. Return to the center of the Temple, and relax forthwith in the completest way possible.

8. Build up the Pyramid

East side of Pyramid YELLOW
South side of Pyramid RED
West side of Pyramid BLUE
North side of Pyramid GREEN
Base side of Pyramid BLACK
Truncated top of Pyramid WHITE

9. Then imagine that you are standing on the top of the Pyramid. You are a vast figure of enormous size perched on an equally large Pyramid, and feel that you are standing on that truncated peak.

10. Then vibrate the Names:

JEHESUAH
JEHOVASHAH

And whilst vibrating the Names, feel yourself being bathed with Light, and that the power is coming through from every part of Space, making you glow with Light.

11. Get off the Pyramid. Wait of course on top, and when you get the impulse to do so, get down. This is a test. I am not telling you what side. You go down to the bottom of the inside of the Pyramid, and remember I am not telling you what side you go into the Pyramid, or what side you go out.

12. Inside the Pyramid you vibrate once more the Divine Names:

JESHSHUAH
JEHOVASHAH
and then four other additional Names. They are four words of five letters each:

EXARP (pronounced X-R-Pay)
HCOMA (pronounced Hay-Co-Mah)
NANTA (pronounced En-En-Tah)
BITOM (pronounced Bay-E-Toe-Em)

These are Enochian Spirit Names.

13. Then wait quietly inside. Do not try to make things happen or formulate things in your imagination. If you get ideas, feelings, or any other concepts, make a mental note of it, and record it in your own notebook or diary at the end of the ritual. Wait quietly for some time until you feel the Meditation has come to an end.

14. Then ascend once more to the top of the Pyramid and feel yourself once more bathed with Light.

15. Then as you stand on the top of the Pyramid, recite the Invocation:

JEHESHUAH, JEHOVASHAH.

I invoke ye, ye Angels of the Celestial Spheres
Whose dwelling is in the invisible.
Ye are the Guardians of the Gates of the Universe.
Be ye also the Guardians of this Mystic Shrine.
Keep far removed the evil and the unbalanced.
Strengthen and inspire me so that I may preserve unsullied
This abode of the Mysteries of the Eternal Gods.
Let my Sphere be pure and holy,
So I may enter in and become a partaker
Of the secrets of the Light Divine. AMEN.

16. Then when you feel you have enough, draw in and perform the Greater Banishing Ritual of the Spirit Pentagram, Active and Passive.

17. Perform the Lesser Banishing Ritual of the Pentagram.

18. Record the result of your Meditation in your notebook or diary.

*Letter to the Editor of*
***THE LONDON FORUM***
by Israel Regardie, December 1933

## NEW MESSIAHS AND EMOTIONAL INTOXICATION

Sir,–What are we to think of the printed slip on the November issue of THE LONDON FORUM bearing the sensational question "Are the Oxford Group and Meher Baba doing the same work?" While one can only trust that the Editorial will succeed in its ostensible project of inducing reflection as to what constitutes true religion and spiritual progress, nevertheless many statements are made which I feel it is imperative to challenge.

It seems to me necessary that we return to fundamental principles. When these are understood, then upon that firm foundation we may safely erect whatever superstructure we contemplate. But basic propositions must first be assimilated thoroughly. Of how many of us may this be said? That even editorial sympathy is wasted in THE LONDON FORUM upon the claims of both the Oxford Group and Meher Baba is proof positive that we must still insist on fundamental propositions.

It is claimed that Meher Baba was able to "extend the consciousness of other individuals at will." The editor asks whether this is self-deception. I do not know, but the question asked in that specific way is certainly no *a priori* reason for assuming that it is not so. Surely he needs no reminder that this failing has not been altogether uncommon in the occult movement–and that most unwittingly. The imputation of worst motives to others does not enter. Because so many thoroughly false and stupid claims are so constantly being made, we must perpetually be alert and on our guard.

The Circle Editorial Committee claims that Baba's purpose is to "revitalize all religions and cults and to bring them together like beads on one string". The Editor compares this with a statement having an almost identical implication issuing from the Oxford Group. Perhaps one may quote from the Introductory to Volume I of Blavatsky's *Secret Doctrine*: "Esoteric Philosophy reconciles all religions, strips every one of its outward human garments, and shows the root of each to be identical with that of every other great religion." Barely forty-five years have elapsed since this was written. All too soon are we looking for saviours–saviours who will relieve us of the necessity of making the supreme effort to discover the God within our inmost souls.

Baba states he has come not to teach, but to awaken. This is all very well, so far as claims go. What are his bona-fides? What has he yet done to differentiate his own mission from the horde of fakirs emanating almost annually from the East. So far reassuring us, nearly everything associated with him arouses intense suspicion and antagonism. His prolonged silence, the alphabet board, innumerable photographs–these are but childish poses. That poses of his description can be associated with spirituality seems to my mind incredible. His journey to America, particularly to Hollywood, where he was to give utterance to his great "message"–what sane comment can one make? It is all so utterly ludicrous. But *reductio ad absurdum* is only too easy. The situation is serious, however, and we must consider these pretensions calmly, for our very interior life is concerned here.

In order to disarm critics, let me state, first of all, though I am proud to call myself a Theosophist, yet I am a member of no Theosophical or other organization. Secondly, I have absolutely nothing against Meher Baba personally. Above all things am I concerned with fundamental philosophical principles at the root of Esotericism–principles, alas, so constantly ignored as to give one the impression that they had never at all been plainly stated in black and white.

True–the world is in a most critical condition both economically and politically, and formal religion is bankrupt. But because this is true let us not be over-anxious to find a too-simple solution to these problems. Do not let us delude ourselves into believing that any one man can "save" the world. It seems that mankind, in spite of authoritative teaching to the contrary, and in spite of common sense, still cherishes the old desire for a Saviour who, by making a vicarious atonement on its behalf, will usher in a new and Golden Age. How soon have we forgotten that progress in self-induced and self-devised! How quickly we have put aside those grand words of the Buddha: "Therefore, o Ananda, be ye lamps unto yourselves. Be ye a refuge to yourselves. Betake yourselves to no external refuge. Hold fast to the truth as a lamp. Hold fast as a refuge to the truth. Look not for refuge to any one besides yourselves."

The statement that Baba will enable mankind to solve "their inner problems by awakening the divine elements within them" is the exact opposite of what the Buddha taught. For the divine elements in man may be awakened only by individual effort, each one for himself, and no miracle-mongering is going to accomplish this enormous and solemn task. Purely on logical tenets of the esoteric philosophy do I doubt that any man may induce in the soul of another a communion with Divinity, or with his own Higher Self. Had that been possible, then centuries ago the great Teachers against whom no conceivable slur can be cast would have accomplished this necessary task of initiation. Compare the statements made, if not by Baba himself then by his disciples, with the principles delineated in *The Mahatma Letters or The Voice of the Silence*. Compare those statements with the teachings of Blavatsky, the unexcelled ethic and spiritual training expounded by the Buddha, and with the system taught by the *Bhagavad Gita*, of self-reliance and attainment through and by self. What then...? I need make no further comment.

Why the Editor expresses that in the activities of the Oxford Group "we have at least something to go on with" surpasses my understanding. Surely for years he has known of the dynamic revivals of the ancient esoteric religions? Has he not himself ably expounded *The Light on the Path* in incomparably fine articles? Were not they "something to get along with"? What the Masters of every age have failed to accomplish is not, *a fortiori*, going to be accomplished by any publicity-seeking messiah, or by an evangelical movement which encourages *emotional intoxication* and a perverse egotistical debauch in the form of public confession.

Let us return or go forward at once to a study of *what* we are, *why* were are here, in what "salvation" or spiritual attainment consists, and cease gadding after every messianic pretender who makes display of occult power.

Yours faithfully,
I. Regardie.

# New Falcon Publications
## Publisher of Controversial Books and CDs
## Invites You to Visit Our Website:
## http://www.newfalcon.com

At the Falcon website you can:

- Browse the online catalog of all our great titles, including books by Robert Anton Wilson, Christopher S. Hyatt, Israel Regardie, Aleister Crowley, Timothy Leary, Osho, Lon Milo DuQuette and many more
- Find out what's available and what's out of stock
- Get special discounts
- Order our titles through our secure online server
- Find products not available anywhere else including:
  – One of a kind and limited availability products
  – Special packages
  – Special pricing
- And much, much more

Get online today at http://www.newfalcon.com

for the transmutation of our personality as into a great Quintessence, for the attainment of the summum bonum, the true Wisdom, the ineffable Beatitude and the term of our quest in Thee. (All officers below give two knocks.)

**Hierophant.**
KHABS

**Hiereus.**
AM

**Hegemon.**
PEKHT

**Hiereus.**
KONX

**Hegemon.**
OM

**Hierophant.**
PAX

**Hegemon.**
Light

**Hierophant.**
In

**Hiereus.**
Extension

(Here ends the Ritual of the Neophyte Grade. Glory be to God in the highest for the mercy he has graciously bestowed upon us.)

communicant in turn. The order of communion is as follows: The Hierophant, the Wardens of the Temple, the Officers of the Temple, excepting the Kerux, who stands at the South of the Altar with the flagon of wine; the Members of the Second Order; outer Members, according to Grade, including the Sentinel; lastly, the Neophyte of the day, who is assisted by the Kerux. When the Neophyte is at the East of the Altar, the Kerux comes to the West and communicates. When handed the Chalice he consumes the wine, and holding the vessel on high he reverses it, and cries with a loud voice.)

**Kerux.**

It is finished. (He replaces the Chalice, raises the Lamp above his head, passes to the East of the Altar, faces East, bends his head before the Hierophant and says:)

**Kerux.**

In the worship of holy conformity and obedience to the Divine Will.

**Hierophant.**

(Knocks twice.) Tetelestai.

**Hiereus.**

(Knocks twice. All give the Signs of the Grade. The Kerux then turns to the West, and having deposited the Lamp, he returns to his place.)

**Hierophant.**

May that which we have received in the body represent in its symbolism to our souls the eternal communication of that life which is above Nature and comes down, O God, from Thee at the close of this solemn office, which we have performed to Thy Glory, that the fulness of Thine efficacious grace may be with us on our going forth into the world, even as on our coming into Thy sanctuary. (He puts down his Sceptre and faces West. All face as before.)

**Hierophant.**

Fratres et Sorores of all Grades in the Order, let us in the bodily communion of sacramental food in common remember that Divine Substance can also be partaken of by the soul. (He goes to the West of the Altar and faces East.)

**Hierophant.**

(Communicating in the bread and salt). Partake with me therefore, I pray you, of this bread ensavoured with salt, as a type of earth. Remember our part of earth and the salt of sanctity which ensavours it. (Raising the Mystical Rose) In breathe with me the fragrance of this Rose, a type of air. Let the images of our understanding and the thoughts of our mind rise as a sweet incense in the sight of God. (Raising the Cup) Drink with me now of this chalice, the consecrated sign of elemental water. (He drinks.) So may our emotions and desires be consecrated and transmuted in God. (Then placing his hands over the fire) And, lastly, let your hands be touched, like my own, by the warmth of this sacred fire, and remember the fire of aspiration which consecrates and changes the will till it is raised from the body of its corruption into living conformity with the Eternal Will.

(He raises the Lamp to his forehead, carries it round with him to the eastern side of the Altar, deposits it in its former place and serves the Imperator of the Temple, raising and handing him each of the elements in turn. This is repeated by each

**Hierophant.**

Let the mystical reverse procession take place in the pathway of the light.

(The Kerux passes from West to South. The Hegemon passes by North to West and South. The Hiereus passes directly to South. The Stolistes passes by West to South. The Dadouchos takes his place on the right of the Stolistes. When the procession is thus formed, the Kerux leads from South to East and all salute in passing the Throne of the Hierophant. When it reaches the Throne of the Hiereus he returns thereto. As it passes the Throne of the Hierophant for the second time the Hegemon retires to his seat. The others circumambulate and salute for the third time, each dropping out as he reaches his own place.)

**Hierophant.**

The mystical reverse procession is accomplished in commemoration of the waning light of Nature and to signify the return of the soul to the material world carrying the symbols of the light. Let us adore the Holy and Eternal God, Who is the Father and the Term of our desires.

(The Hierophant descends from his Throne and faces the East thereat. All turn East, maintaining the Sign of the Grade until the adoration is over.)

**Hierophant.**

O Thou has called Thy servants in all generations and hast set apart Thine elect to Thy service, who hast filled our hearts with the aspiration towards Thy union, and all Thy channels of grace with the means of its attainment: Give us this day and forever our daily desire for Thee, and grant, we beseech Thee,

**Hiereus.**

Fratres et Sorores, give me the outward signs which are attributed to the First Grade of the light within. (This being done.) Truly Honoured Hierophant, they have seen His star in the East and have come to adore Him. (The first Sign is here given by the Hiereus and the second by the Hierophant.)

**Hierophant.**

May the Angel of Great Counsel and the prince of Peace and the Light which enlighteneth every man who cometh into this world, give us grace and illumination in our day. Let the Temple be cleansed with water and consecrated by fire, to symbolise the purification that is within.

(The Stolistes follows the course of the sun, coming eastward from his place in the North. He makes a Cross with his cup and sprinkles thrice in the East. He performs the same ceremony in the other quarters and returns to the East, where he again faces the Hierophant, raises the Cup of Water, and says:)

**Stolistes.**

Waters of Understanding, Waters of the Great Sea: I have purified with water.

(He salutes the Throne and returns to his place by South and West. The Dadouchos follows, observing the same procedure with his Vessel of Incense. Having returned to the East, he says, raising the Turible:)

**Dadouchos.**

The desire of the House of the Lord hath eaten me up: I have consecrated with fire. (He salutes the Throne and returns.)

## THE SOLEMN CEREMONY OF CLOSING THE TEMPLE IN THE NEOPHYTE GRADE

(The Sentinel having left the Temple: Without any other admonition on the part of the Hierophant, the Kerux proceeds to the place of proclamation in the usual manner and raises his Lamp and Wand.)

**Kerux.**

Hekas, Hekas, este bebeloi. (He returns to his place with the Sun.)

**Hierophant.**

Fratres et Sorores, in the banishment of all earthly thoughts and in the recollection of the heart, assist me to close the Temple in the Grade of Neophyte. (All rise.)

**Hierophant.**

Let the keeper of the Holy Place on the hither side of the Portal ascertain that the Temple is guarded.

(The Kerux gives one knock on the hither side of the door. The Sentinel responds in the same manner on the outer side, using the hilt of his sword.)

**Kerux.**

Truly Honored Hierophant, on the hither and further side it is firmly guarded.

**Hierophant.**

Fratres et Sorores, lift up your hearts. I testify on my part that the world is still without and the prince thereof. Honourable Frater Hiereus, assure yourself that all present have seen the Golden Dawn, which is a light in the inmost heart.

of the mind, and our hearts with that fire which being enkindled on earth shall in the end carry us to heaven.

We are dealing, Brethren, and shall continue to deal henceforward, not alone with the question of religion, but with its heart and centre behind all the external differences of systems and churches and sects. The Grades of the Order of the Golden Dawn are the grades of our progression in God, and in these–as in those which we take in that other and not less symbolical progression of daily life–it rests with us whether they shall remain symbolism or whether we shall pass in them, and they shall pass in us, into the actual region of experience. It is because of that infinite realm which lies behind the woven circle of official religion that you are counselled in this Grade to respect the forms thereof. The external churches are doors which open for many if not indeed for you, and there is perchance one of them which for you also may open, into the places of peace, into the light which is fine will enlighten every man who comes into this world. Looking unto which region, and remembering the term of our desire, let us pray that we all who are inheritors of a dying world may enter into another heritage in the world without end. (The Minutes of the previous Meeting and the other official business, if any, are taken at this point.)

And now as regards the experience through which you have just passed, we have no occasion to remind you that in the physical order we come forth from darkness into light, and that in the intellectual order most comparisons between light and darkness are an economy of our real meaning. The progress of the Candidate from the one to the other state in the Grade of Neophyte is understood among us in a particular sense, which at the same time has a certain natural analogy with the more usual meaning. The birth of the soul in our consciousness is like birth into physical life. As the life of the Candidate anteceded his reception into the Order, so the soul which is within us antecedes that moment when it issues, as it were, from its concealment within us and begins to manifest by its operation. This is the beginning of the supernatural life, of the life of grace and hereof is the whole Grade a symbol. When the desire of the House of the Lord awakens within us, our passage from darkness has already begun; we have been called to the Living Beauty; that which is termed among us the Lamp of the Hidden Knowledge has been uplifted and proceeds before us on the way; it is the experience of those who are our precursors in the ascent of the Holy Mountain. Through the keen air of high aspiration, as in the uplifted region of the mind, may we pass into that world of flame, wherein are the Sons and Daughters of Desire! When desire and aspiration have attained their term in us, may there be communicated at length that bread and even that salt which are types of the earth no longer but the food of souls! May we drink of that wine reserved for those who are athirst in the Kingdom of our Father! The lustrations are many, and the consecrations also are many looking for that time when God shall cleanse us from our sins with living water, pouring through the chambers

## THE ALLOCUTION

**Hierophant.**

Fratres et Sorores, holding all Grades of the Order, by the power to me transmitted from the Wardens of this Temple, I invite you to hear with recollected hearts the Allocution belonging to the Grade of Neophyte. And you, our Brother, who have been received this day among us, to you we address more especially these few words, which, we trust, will abide in your memory and will perform their office within you to your own and to our advantage. We have invoked upon you the Morning Redness, Gold of Morning, even the Extended Light, and we feel that within the peaceful abode of this Order you may find not only an abode of spiritual contemplation apart from the outer world of our daily solicitude, but a sanctuary where the symbols of the secret knowledge may bring to you some radiance or reflection of the direct Light which shines in the Temple of Light–that Temple which is not entered with earthly feet or seen with the veiled eyes of this body of our mortality. We trust also that the Order may become to you one of those hearths and homes around which the love of brotherhood is gathered–that love which does not fail us in the hour of inward need. In this respect we are pledged to you whom we have admitted, as you are pledged to us: we ask you to remember this, as we also remember, and among the last things which we can offer to you at this time is the maxim in chief of fraternity founded on consanguinity of spirit; Brother, the keys of all the greater mysteries are committed to the hands of love.

that things Divine are not for those who understand the body alone. Remember that many burdens are cast aside on the path upward, and that only those who are lightly clothed will attain to the summit. Remember the charity of the wise and respect the religions which are sacred to those about you, for there are many paths to the centre. Remember the law of equilibrium and learn by its help to distinguish between the good and evil, to choose the one and put aside the other, until that time comes when goodness shall fill the heart entirely. Remember lastly that steadfastness prevails over all difficulties, and do not be daunted by those which await you in the pursuit of that Hidden Knowledge of which God is the motive and the end.

**Hierophant.**

The titles of your advancement to the next Grade of the Order depend in part on yourself and in part on us. Ponder over that which is communicated in the Portal of the Secret Light. In such reflection and in the examination of your own conscience you will find a further light, and that light is your warrant. The instruction which we offer for your guidance may be obtained on application to the Cancellarius, but your advancement itself can take place only by the dispensation of the Second Order. (The Allocution of the Neophyte Grade then follows, and may be delivered by the Hierophant or one of the Wardens of the Temple.)

**Hierophant.**

Frater Kerux, you have my command to proclaim that the Neophyte has entered the Portal and has been admitted into the mysteries of the Neophyte Grade in the Holy Order of the Golden Dawn. (The Kerux passes by West to North, and standing at the right hand but to the front of the Hierophant, and facing West, he raises his Lamp and Wand.)

**Kerux.**

In the Name of God who is our Light, and by the ordinance of the Truly Honoured Hierophant, hear ye all: I proclaim and testify that A.B., who will be known hence forth among us by the sacramental title of Frater (vel Soror) Adveniat Regnum (vel alius), has passed the Portal of the Golden Dawn and has been admitted to the Mysteries of the Neophyte Grade. (He returns to his place with the Sun.)

**Hiereus.**

Frater Adveniat Regnum (vel alius), I exhort you to keep in everlasting memory the obligation to secrecy which you have taken on your entrance into this Order. Regard it as a test of merit, and its faithful observance as a title of salvation, a warrant for our advancement in the soul. There is strength in silence, the seed of Wisdom is sown therein and it grows in darkness and mystery. Remember the Mystery which you have received; it is the shadow of a greater Mystery, whereof tongue cannot speak. Honour God who is our light. From Him proceeds all things and unto Him all things return. Continue to desire that Divine Vision which you are pledged to seek. Remember that those who go before you may place in the path of its attainment, but the soul must ascend of itself till the grace and the power come down and abide in its secret sanctuary. Remember and that is purity, which is symbolised by his white robe. It is in and by this quality that he directs the higher aspirations of the spirit. Purity is not only the condition, but in a sense it is also the term; it is not only the first link in the chain which leads from earth to heaven, but it is the chain itself. It is the Ladder of Jacob, by which the aspirations ascend and the great influences come down. It is said that Religion pure and undefiled before God and the Father is this: To visit the fatherless and the widowed in their affliction and to keep oneself unspotted from the world. The Hegemon coming forth from between the Pillars, and going even outside the door of the Temple into the place of the uniniated, is sent to save that which is in dereliction. His ministry is to those who are widowed of the Divine Spouse and to those who are fatherless, being without God in the world. When he goes out therefore, it is as if a voice said: and God so loved the world.

But the qualities and graces and virtues which are represented by the chief officers are in a state of superincession. There is also a sense in which the Hierophant and Hiereus both represent the love that is behind the universe, in virtue of the correspondences of which it is possible for God to be so near the heart of man that it is more easy to attain than to miss Him. This is why the path upward is natural and straight in comparison with the path downward.

In respect of the lesser officers, you have heard what is symbolised by the Lamp and Function of the Kerux. He is the light of the end which goes before the cohorts of salvation. The Stolistes and Dadouchos, who are seated in the South and North, carry the outward signs of the things which purify within. It is in virtue of such lustrations and such consecrations that the Candidate comes at length to the East, as the quest to its term and desire to its proper attainment. (A pause.)

Ritual of the Dead. They are symbols of eternal equilibrium, active and passive, fixed and volatile, severity and mercy. The solid triangles on their summits bear each a veiled lamp, signifying the triad of life. Between them lies the narrow path of the Hidden Wisdom. It was down this path, my brother, that I passed for your reintegration in the light; on the threshold thereof, and between the Two Pillars, you received the secrets of the Grade, the distinguishing badge and the final and perfect consecration.

You should now learn that the Hierophant on his Throne in the East personifies the substance and the evidence and the experience which are represented by faith in the eternal. He is the Rising Sun in Nature and power, light, mercy and wisdom in the providential world. It is said: Ex oriente Lux, and that light is for the illumination of the peoples of the earth. Behold He hath placed His Tabernacle in the sun, and the purpose is that our feet may be directed in the way of peace. This is how the Orient from on high visits us. The intention is furthermore that the knowledge of salvation may be granted to His people. This is the import of the power of the Hierophant and the correspondence thereof is His mercy, for mercy is on all sides. But the correspondence of his light is his wisdom, and this wisdom symbolises that what proceeds from the mouth of the Most High, reaching from end to end and strongly and sweetly overruling all things. The Hierophant is also the teaching spirit at the place of the Rending of the Veil.

The Hegemon represents religion, the foundation of which is in faith, but it is also holy hope. He is the Mediator, the Reconciler, the Preparer for the Path to the Divine. He represents in an especial manner the condition of the ascent of the soul, burning coal. The cross-marking with lustral water and the mystic sprinkling showed forth sacramentally the condition on which your name is registered in the Book of Life. The Altar at which you knelt is in the form of a double cube, with its base of necessity concealed, the surfaces exposed to sight, while on the summit are the sacred emblems whereon you were pledged and whereby you are bound in the sight of God henceforth and forever. The Altar is black to portray the state of our natural humanity and the darkness of the uninformed world before the Word of creative light went forth therein. That Word is typified by the White Triangle which is placed on the Altar; it is the sign of Divine Immanence in Nature; and also of that which must be declared in your soul, my brother, for the manifestation of the Divine therein. At the apex of the White Triangle, there is placed a Red Cross, which is the sign of Him who is unfolded in light through the universe and through the soul is grace. (The Hierophant rises and extends his arms in the form of a cross.)

**Hierophant.**

Thanks be to Thee, O Lord and Father Almighty, for the Secret Word which is conceived and born in the heart. We have accepted Thy Cross and Thy Calvary because of the glorious resurrection that is to come. May Thy World also be born in the heart of this Neophyte. May it grow in grace and truth. May the power and perfection of its fulness be as the glory of the King of all. (The Hierophant resumes his seat.)

**Hierophant.**

To the East of the Cubical Altar are the Pillars which are analogically referred to Seth, Hermes and Solomon as allusions to the secret tradition and its perpetuation by the guardians of the Mysteries. They bear certain hieroglyphical texts from the

**Hierophant.**

You will now take your seat as an approved and received Neophyte on the northern side of the Temple and toward the West.

(The Hiereus restores the Sceptre to the Hegemon. The Hegemon passes round the White Pillar, leads the Neophyte with the sun to his assigned place, and returns to his own between the Pillars, where his seat is restored. This completes the ceremonial part of the reception. The Kerux replaces the Rose replaces the Rose, Lamp, Chalice and Paten on the Altar. All Officers are seated.)

**Hierophant.**

Frater Adveniat Regnum (vel alius), the Order of the Golden Dawn extends to you its loving welcome on your admission as a Neophyte of this Temple. May there be joy in the blessed Hierarchies at your coming out of earthly into spiritual life, and may that joy in its reflection fall like the rain of love into your heart of hearts. Your preparation as a Candidate was in the body, to symbolise that greater preparation which you had already made in your heart before you could be accepted as a Postulant. The triple cord which was placed about you represented the threefold bondage of your mortality, and when it was in fine loosed this signified the liberation of your higher part. The sacramental title which you have assumed in place of your earthly designation is a token of our Secret Name in the Temple that is above: it is the nearest that you can reach in your aspiration to that which in this life is hidden even from yourself. The hoodwink imaged the darkness of the material mind. The censing in your several consecrations prefigured the cleansing with fire from the Supernal Altar of Incense. May your heart and your reins be purified thereby as if with a

(The Stolistes and Dadouchos, following the course of the sun, come forward successively from their places. They raise their vessels of consecration before the Hierophant, then turn and consecrate the Neophyte, saying:)

**Stolistes.**
In the Name of the Fountain of Living Water which purifies the will of man. I consecrate you with Water.

**Dadouchos.**
In the name of the Divine Desire which redirects the will of man, I consecrate you with Fire. (Again saluting the Throne, they return to their places.)

**Hierophant.**
Honourable Frater Hegemon, let the Neophyte be unbound between the Pillars, to symbolise the transmutation of the lower parts of the personality, so that they may concur in the work of the will when the will has been turned to the light. (This is done accordingly, the Sceptre of the Hegemon being taken in charge by the Hiereus.)

**Hierophant.**
Let our Frater be also invested with the Mystic Badge of this Grade. (The Neophyte is invested with the Ribbon, and this completes the ceremonial part of his reception. The silent circumambulation in the light which used to take place at this point has no authority in the Cipher MSS. It was preceded by a simple direction on the part of the Hierophant.)

**Hegemon.**
By command of the Truly Honoured Hierophant, receive the Badge of this Grade: the prevailing colour is black, representing darkness, but the Light of the Eternal Triad is dawning therein.

advancing your (he is given instruction), as I advance my own. The signs are called respectively those of (again instruction is given) and of (again instruction is given), and the second is the answer to the first. The Sign of (again instruction is given), and the second is the answer to the first. The Sign of (again instruction is given) is given by putting out the (again instruction is given), the (again instruction is given) being also inclined. In this position you are as one (again instruction is given) and it is intended to remind you of that state in which you came among us but recently, seeking and asking for the light. The Sign of Silence refers to your solemn covenant. The Token or Grip is given (again instruction is given. The Hiereus maintains the Grip.) It recalls your search for guidance in the darkness. In this position the syllables of the Word are exchanged in an undertone. It is (again instruction is given), the Egyptian name of the God of Silence. The temporal Password of the Order is changed at each Equinox; at the present time it is (again instruction is given). I now place you between the Symbolic Pillars at the Gateway of Hidden Wisdom.

(He draws the Neophyte forward by the Grip of the Grade, taking care that he does not cross the threshold represented by the two Pillars. He resumes his station by the Black Pillar.)

**Hierophant.**
Honourable Frater Hiereus, I bid you remember that behind the will of man is the Portal of the Supreme Mystery.

**Hiereus.**
Truly Honoured Hierophant, in commemoration of that Mystery, and in obedience to your ordinance, I demand the final and perfect consecration.

**Hierophant.**

When the guiding hands led you in the dark circle of your wanderings, the Light of the Hidden Wisdom went before you, symbolised by the Lamp of the Kerux. Know and remember henceforward that this wisdom, which begins in the fear of the Lord ends at his Palace at the centre. (All officers return to their stations except the Hegemon.)

**Hierophant.**

Let the Neophyte be led to the eastern side of the Altar; let him stand with his face to the East. (The Hegemon leads accordingly by North to East and places the Neophyte in the middle way between the Altar and the Pillars.)

**Hierophant.**

Honourable Frater Hiereus, you will now impart to the Neophyte the Secret Signs, Tokens and Word which are allocated to the 0-0 Grade in the Portal of the Golden Dawn. You will also communicate the temporal password which is common to the whole Order.

(The Hiereus passes form his Throne by North to the Black Pillar and stands on its Eastern side, facing South. The Hegemon leaves the Neophyte, and passing by North takes up a similar position before the White Pillar, but facing towards the North. The Sword of the Hiereus is sheathed. The Hiereus turns West and faces the Neophyte. He stands between the Pillars.)

**Hiereus.**

Frater Adveniat Regnum (vel aliud), by the decree of the Truly Honoured Hierophant, receive at my hands the Secret Signs, Token and Word of the Portal. The step is given by

**Hierophant.**
The emblems of High Light are restored to the Novice.

**Hierophant.**
KHABS.

**Hiereus.**
AM

**Hegemon.**
PEKHT

**Hiereus.**
KNOX

**Hegemon.**
OM

**Hierophant.**
PAX

**Hegemon.**
Light

**Hierophant.**
In

**Hiereus.**
Extension

(The three Chief Officers remove their Sceptres and Sword from above the head of the Candidate. The Kerux passes to North-East of the Altar and raises his Lamp. The Hierophant points thereto.)

Novice), place them in humility and reverence on our Altar of Sacrifice. (The Novice is directed to clasp his hands over the Altar.)

**Hierophant.**
O Thou Who sanctifiest the heart of man. Who leadest our desires into attainment and our aspirations to the steps of Thy House, sanctify, Eternal God, this Novice of our Order. Lead him to the perfection which is in Thee, into the splendour of Thy great White Throne. May that which here and now I restore to him in the outward signs of Thy most blessed sacraments and Thine all-sacred symbols be ratified above in Thy presence and realised essentially within him, to the glory of Thy Name, world without end, Amen and to the joy of Thy redeemed Hierarchies.

(The Novice is assisted to rise. The Hierophant comes close to the Altar and lifts his Sceptre respectively to touch the Sceptre of the Hierophant.)

**Hegemon.**
Thou who wouldst be saved and hast come out of the ways of darkness, enter into thy holy inheritance.

**Hiereus.**
Thou in whom the world has not anything from henceforth and forever, come into the Holy Light. (At the word Light the Kerux finally removes the hoodwink and the Sentinel turns up the lights.)

**Hierophant.**
We receive thee into the place of our sacraments, among the signs without the things that are realised within, into the pure and shining mystery, into the Order of the Golden Dawn.

**Hierophant.**

The Mystery of Eternal Light dawning in the darkness of material things, and communicate to the soul of man, is declared in the East of the Temple. I am the Light enkindled, the Morning Light, the desire of the eyes of the world. I am the Expounder of Mysteries. I am love and immortality and the hope of the Kingdom in its coming. I am the Guardian of the Veil and I speak in the opening of the eyes, proclaiming the path of wisdom and the secret law of equilibrium.

(The hoodwink is again replaced over the eyes of the Novice and the procession passes to the Altar. The Hierophant leaves his Throne, bearing his Sceptre. He stops (a) between the Pillars, (b) half-way between these and the Altar, or (c) close to the eastern side of the Altar. The Hiereus comes forward to his place on the North side in the angle towards the West. The Hegemon places the Novice in the West and moves to the South side in the angle towards the West. The Kerux stands at a little distance behind the Novice. The Stolistes and Dadouchos stand due East of the Hiereus and Hegemon, respectively. Wherever the Hierophant pauses, he says slowly and clearly:)

**Hierophant.**

I come in the power of the light; I come in the Light of Wisdom; I come in the mercy of the light. The light has healing in its wings. (And afterwards at the East of the Altar:)

**Hierophant.**

Behold, I stand at all thy doors and knock. Open thy heart, O Novice of this Order. Take in thy hand the desires and aspirations which have brought thee to our Holy Temple, and kneeling with bowed head (the Hegemon and Kerux here assist the

**Kerux.**

The desires and emotions of the natural man are a sea in torment: unpurified and unconsecrated, their place is not found by the Throne of the Throne of the Temple in the East. (The Stolistes cross-marks as before.)

**Stolistes.**

In the Name of the Fountain of Living Water which cleanses the heart of man, I purify you with Water. (The Dadouchos ceses as before.)

**Dadouchos.**

In the Name of the Divine Desire which converts the heart of man, I consecrate you with fire.

**Hegemon.**

Son of the night and time, thrice washed with Holy Water and purged by consecrated Fire, your way is free in the East.

(The Kerux leads the procession to the Throne of the Hierophant. The Hegemon leads up the Novice and raises his hoodwink, so that he sees the Hierophant, standing with uplifted Sceptre, holding the Banner of the East.)

**Hierophant.**

You cannot pass by me, says the Guardian of the East, until you have learned my Name.

**Hegemon.**

(On the part of the Novice.) You are Light in the place of Light. Light dawning in Darkness for the liberation and salvation of those who dwell in the House of Bondage and in the Shadow of Death.

**Hegemon.**

Son of the night and time, twice washed with holy water and purged by consecrated fire, your way is free in the West.

(The procession pauses at the Throne of the Hiereus, who knocks once. The Kerux faces him on the right hand. The Hegemon leads up the Novice and raises his hoodwink. The Hiereus stands with drawn Sword holding the Banner of the West.)

**Hiereus.**

You cannot pass by me, says the Guardian of the West, until you have learned my Name.

**Hegemon.**

(On the part of the Novice). You are darkness in the place of darkness, questioning the Seekers of the Light.

**Hiereus.**

The Mystery of the Presence in the West is declared at the Gate of the Temple for the encouragement of reconciled souls. I am the protection from the evil that is within you. I am Divine Fortitude. I am Judgment, by which the good is set apart from the evil. I am the Providence which works in darkness. Go forward and fear not, for he who is established in God does not tremble at the flame or at the flood, or at the inconstant shadows of the air.

(The Hegemon replaces the hoodwink; the procession moves forward till it arrives again at the North. The Kerux, turning, bars the way for the second time. The Stolistes and Dadouchos come forward as before.)

procession. The Stolistes and Dadouchos occupy the third line. The procession moves slowly, with great reverence and in the utmost silence, except at the stated points of the liturgy. The Hierophant knocks once as it passes the East. The Kerux halts in the South, the Stolistes and Dadouchos divide, passing one on each side of the Hegemon and Novice, till they are in front of the Kerux. All turn and the Kerux bars the way with his Wand. The Cipher MSS. from which this Ritual depends indicate only one circumambulation of the Temple at this point; it has been customary to triple it in practice. The first circumambulation was in silence, except for one battery of the Hiereus; at the second the Hierophant knocked once, the consecration took place in the South, and the Novice was taken to the Hiereus; the third completed the procedure at the North and East as above. The innovation has no authority, but is justified by convenience in a small Temple.)

**Kerux.**

The thought of the natural mind are unpurified and unconsecrated; their place is not found by the Throne of the West. (The Stolistes cross-marks the Novice on the forehead and sprinkles three times.)

**Stolistes.**

In the Name of the Fountain of Living Water which cleanses the thought of man, I purify you with Water. (The Dadouchos makes a Cross with Thurible and censes three times.)

**Dadouchos.**

In the Name of the Divine Desire which transmutes the thought of man, I consecrate you with fire. (The Stolistes and Dadouchos fall back to their places in the rear.)

**Hierophant.**
Rise, Novice of the Portal Grade in the Order of the Golden Dawn. (The Novice is assisted accordingly. The Hierophant and Hiereus return to their places. All members are seated.)

**Hierophant.**
Being mindful, O Honourable Hegemon, that all things are within–all joys, all dangers, all hopes, all fears, with the ways of the height and deep–let the Novice be placed in the northern part of the Temple, to symbolise the state of spiritual coldness, the night of the human mind and of grace inhibited. (This is done accordingly, but the Novice is faced to the East.)

**Hierophant.**
I asked to be taken from the darkness and holy hands led me in the covert of holy wings. I asked to be brought into the light, and the loving wings were closed about the face of me, lest I should see God and die. I asked to kneel at the steps of the Throne of God and they set me in the Holy Place, even by the Tabernacle. O God, how wonderfully is Thy work declared in the heart of man: I will walk in Thy ways forever. (A pause.)

**Hierophant.**
Let the Novice be led from the darkness and through the darkness toward the Light by a symbolical advancement on the faith of his intention. Let the outward symbol of the inward light go before him, like the destiny of attainment before those who are born for the light.

(The Dadouchos passes by West to North, and when he has paused on the right of the Stolistes, the Kerux takes his place in front of the Hegemon and Novice and goes before the

I promise solemnly from this moment that I will persevere with courage and devotion in the path of Divine Science, even as I shall persevere undaunted through this ceremony which is its image, and whatsoever I may learn or attain in this Temple and in the Order, I will receive as from the hands of God and to His hands will return it in purity. I certify hereby and heron that I desire above all things the grace of the secret knowledge, but since that knowledge is also power, I convenant that at no time and under no temptation will apply it to the works of evil. I will hold myself dedicated henceforth, so far as in me lies, to the consecration of my outward and inward nature, that I may deserve to leave the darkness and to dwell in the world of light. I will abide with my brethren in union, rectitude and purity, remembering that peace is in God. Bending over this holy symbol of light dawning in the soul, I swear to observe all parts and points of this pledge without evasion, equivocation, or mental reservation of any kind, praying as I deal herein in all high faith and honour that my secret name may be written in the Book of Life, even as its symbol will be registered this day in the Books of the Order. I invoke upon my own head the penalty of expulsion from the Order if ever I am wilfully guilty of perjury herein. May I go in fear of the second death, the change of the Infinite Benignity into Divine wrath and of the Divine Will into a hostile current which shall paralyse the life of the soul. Deal with me, O Lord, in Thy mercy; strengthen my heart and my reins; for even as I bow my neck under the Sword of the Hiereus (it is placed on the neck of the Candidate), so do I commit myself into Thy hands for judgment or reward. So help me my mighty and secret soul; so help me the sun of my soul; enlighten me in the dark places and bring me at last to Thee. (A pause.)

this Order, that it may be married to the sincerity and holiness which abide in its own heart. Bow your head, as one who has come out of the world looking for those gifts that do not belong to the world. For the first and last time in the presence of this Assembly, recite your earthly name and say after me:

**Hierophant.**
(Followed by Candidate) I, A.B., in the presence of the Eternal Father of Light, who recompenses those who seek Him out, in the presence of the Brethren who are gathered here together in the grace of His Divine Name, do of my own will and in the consciousness of my proper act and deed, submitted in conformity with the act and will of God, most solemnly pledge the honour of my soul to keep inviolable the secrets of this Temple and of the Mysteries which are worked within it. I will not speak of them in the world without, when I go forth therein. I will not disclose the name of this Temple or Order, or the name of any of its members. I will not reveal the knowledge communicated to me therein. I will keep the secrets of the Sanctuary as I would keep those of my King and God, speaking to me in the inmost places of the soul. I will conform to the Laws of the Order and to the By-Laws of this Temple. I will have no part or dealing with respect of this Order, its Rites, Proceedings, or its Knowledge, with any member who has been cast out therefrom, nor will I recognise the living membership of any person who is not in possession of the temporal Password communicate at each Equinox to the recognised Temples. I hereby include within the category of this sacred pledge whatever information I may have received concerning the Order prior to my admission therein. I lift up my heart to God Who is my Judge, and seeing that I have come hither actuated by the most solemn motives which are conceived by the soul of man,

mortality and the code of society to keep the laws of both, so you must be covenanted herein to keep the rule of the Temple and never to disclose without that which you learn within. But it is just, on our part, to assure you, as I now do in God's Name, that the pledge which we exact does in no wise derogate from the laws of man but leads to their better fulfilment in the light of Divine law. Are you willing to take this meet and salutary Obligation? (The Candidate is prompted by the Hegemon.)

**Candidate.**
I desire the light of the House, and I take its laws upon me. (The Hierophant, in conformity with the symbolism, comes down from his Throne and goes to the East of the Altar, saying:)

**Hierophant.**
It is written that I will visit the heart of men, for my delight is in the way of justice.

(He stands facing to the West. The Hiereus comes to the North side of the Altar and the Hegemon to the South side. The three Officers thus form a triangle, and the Candidate, who is close to the Altar on the western side, is joined therein at the middle point of the base. The Members of all Grades rise and remain standing while the Obligation is taken.)

**Hierophant.**
Postulant in the Home of the Spirit, looking for grace to come, in the Name of the Lord of Grace. Who is the Fountain of all our light, I bid you kneel down as a sign of your humility and obedience. (The Candidate is assisted to kneel.) Give me your right hand, which I impose on this holy sign of light shining in the darkness; place your left hand in mine, as a pledge of the sacred and sincere intention which your heart brings into

(He falls back. The Dadouchos comes forward, raises his Thurible before the face of the Candidate, makes the Sign of the Cross therewith and censes him three times.)

**Hierophant.**
Inheritor of night and time, child of the material world, what seek you in the places of the soul?

**Hegemon.**
(Replying for Candidate). Through the darkness of time and night, I have come to the Gate of the Temple, looking for the light within.

**Hierophant.**
Place the Postulant at the western side of the Altar with his face to the East, symbolising the desire after that light which God shall grant to the seeker who is well and properly prepared. (This is done by the Hegemon, who leads the Candidate helpfully and carefully throughout the Ceremony. He is not allowed to kneel, to rise, or to move of his own accord.)

**Hierophant.**
We hold your signed application for admission to this Order, which exists for the communication of spiritual knowledge to those how have awakened in the spirit. We hold also your solemn testimony to a desire conceived in your heart for the grace of Eternal Life and Divine Union. We are taught that the things which are Caesar's must be rendered duly to Caesar but to God the things that are God's, and the secrets of the Sanctuary are reserved to the Sanctuary alone. Before your reception can proceed, it is necessary for you to take a solemn Obligation to maintain the Veils of the Order, and as in the world without you are bound by the canons of

(The Stolistes, moving by North and East, joins Dadouchos in the South, and they proceed together to the door. The lights are turned down. The Kerux opens the door, and taking up his place about five feet within, he bars the further progress of the Candidate when he has entered the Portal. Behind him stand the Stolistes and Dadouchos. As he leads the Candidate:)

**Hegemon.**
The darkness is also God's minister. The darkness shall lead His servant.

**Dadouchos.**
The Treasure of the Hidden Fire shall shine therein.

**Stolistes.**
It is over the Great Sea and in the deeps thereof.

**Hierophant.**
The night shall be enlightened with the day. (The Hegemon again advances, leading the Candidate. The Kerux bars the way.)

**Kerux.**
The things that are holy are reserved for those that are holy and the sanctuary of initiation for consecrated and initiated men. Son (and Daughter) of the Night and Time, and child of Earth, you cannot enter the Temple of Sacred Mystery. (The Stolistes comes forward, cross-marks the Candidate on the forehead and sprinkles three times before him.)

**Stolistes.**
In the Name of the Foundation of Living Water, which cleanses the Children of Earth, I purify you with water.

loaded in his exile, far from the home of the heart. He cannot walk alone and hence he so depends upon our guidance. He will not be deserted in his need. He will be brought safely and surely into the secret place of our light. There is faith and there is hope in his heart, and that which leads him in the narrow way is the hand of love. (The preparation being over, the Hegemon gives an alarm of a knock at the outer side of the Portal. The Kerux replies with a knock.)

**Kerux.**
Truly Honoured Hierophant, the Mediator between light and darkness, the Lord of Reconciliation and Peace, stands at the door without.

**Hierophant.**
Do you certify, Frater Kerux, that he returns in the name of his mission, for the fulfilment of a work of redemption?

**Kerux.**
He will only that it should be accomplished.

**Hierophant.**
God made the world without, as He made that which is within. May the Peace of the Lord fill those who are seeking His light. I give you permission to admit A.B., who puts aside henceforth in these precincts his earthly title and dignities and receives at our hands that name which represents his aspiration on entering here among us. He will be known hereafter as Frater Adveniat Regnum (vel aliud), and may he that enters the Kingdom receive the crown of all. Fratres Dadouchos et Stolistes, in the purifying sign of fire and the holy water of regeneration, be ready to receive the Candidate.

## THE CEREMONIAL ADMISSION OF A NEOPHYTE IN THE PORTAL OF THE GOLDEN DAWN

(The Kerux removes the Rose, Lamp, Chalice and Paten from the Altar.)

**Hierophant.**

Fratres et Sorores, I beseech you to lift up your hearts to prayer that the Divine Assistance may be with us efficiently in the work which I am delegated to perform as an authorised Expounder of the Mysteries. I have received a Dispensation from the Concealed Superiors of the Order to admit A.B. to the first circle of initiation in the Portal of the Golden Dawn. I command therefore the Honourable Frater Hegemon to take in charge the preparation of the Postulant and to see that the things within are symbolised by the things without.

(The Hegemon rises, removes his seat from the middle place of the Pillars to a convenient point left free for this purpose, and having reached the hither side of the door, he turns eastward, makes with recollection the Side of a Neophyte and then passes without the Portal. He prepares the Candidate by placing a hoodwink over his eyes and a threefold cord about his body. While this is being done:)

**Hierophant.**

The things that are without are in analogy with the things that are within. The eyes of our Postulant at the Gate of the Mysteries are darkened for a period, to symbolise the cloud that rests upon the sanctuary of his soul. The body of our Postulant is bound, to typify the material chain with which he has been reverence for the mysteries that are about to be performed. I go before the Candidate, as God goes before the elect on the path of their return to Him. (The Lamp is lowered. The Hegemon uplifts his Sceptre.)

**Hegemon.**

I am the Mediator and Reconciler, the preparer of the pathway to the Divine. My seat is between the Pillars and I preside over the Gate of the Mysteries. I am the condition of the ascent of the soul, which is the purity symbolised by my white robe. I am the peace of the equalibrium which reconciles light and darkness. I direct in virtue of purity the higher aspirations of the soul. I am religion, which manifests in benignity, and the middle way by which ascent is possible to the light. I carry a mitre-headed Sceptre, which represents the sacramental side of holy churches and creeds. In virtue of this my office and of its high symbolism, I am the leader of the Candidate in all Grades of the Order and I direct him in the true way. (The Sceptre of the Hegemon is lowered. The Hiereus draws and raises his Sword. He raises the Banner of the West.)

**Hiereus.**

I am set upon the Throne of the West. I symbolise external darkness. I cast out the images of matter. I am the spirit which clears the obsessions. I am called Fortitude in the Mysteries, but my fortitude and refuges are Thee, O God. I am the protection from the evil within the Candidate. I carry the Sword of Judgment and the Banner of the Evening Twilight. I announce that which I represent at the gate of entrance to the heights. (The Hiereus replaces his Banner. He sheathes his Sword. The Hierophant raises his own Sceptre and Banner.)

**Dadouchos.**

My place is the South of the Temple and I bear the thurible of my office. I represent material heat manifesting in the outer world and the fire that is communicated within. In respect of that fire it is said: My soul hath thirsted for the Lord, in the pathless and waterless respect of that fire it is said: My soul hath thirsted for the Lord, in the pathless and waterless desert of this world. I symbolise the desire of God which has burnt up all earthly roses and has wasted all the false gardens of delight, so that the soul can find neither food nore wine therein. I am the heat of that supernatural fire which consumes all lusts of the flesh, lusts of the eye and pride of life. It is in this sense that I consecrate the Candidate with the fire. (The Thurible is lowered. The Stolistes, standing in his place, raises the cup of water.)

**Stolistes.**

My place is in the North of the Temple and I bear the water of my office. I represent material cold and moisture manifesting in the outer world and the waters of the fountain of salvation that pour upon the world within. I am the other side of the Divine desire, for even as the hart panteth after the water-brooks so doth the soul of man desire after Thee, O God. It is in this sense the ! purify the Candidate with water. (The Cup of water is lowered. The Kerux, standing in his place at the northern side of the Hiereus, raises his Lamp.)

**Kerux.**

My place is on the hither side of the Portal. I carry the Lamp of my office, which symbolises material light shining in the outer world but more especially the secret light which dawns in the world of grace. I make all official announcement; I report to the Hierophant of the Temple; I lead circumambulations; and I see that the Temple is prepared in piety and whereof they are images may be quickened in the spheres of those who are here and now present and in the perfect sphere of the Order. Honourable Frater Hiereus, how many are the principal officers of the Neophyte Grade?

**Hiereus.**

As in all Grades and Degrees of the Outer Order, they reflect by their triplicity below the Eternal Triad which is above: they are the Hierophant, the Hiereus and the Hegemon.

**Hierophant.**
What have these titles in common?

**Hiereus.**
The letter H, symbol of breath and life.

**Hierophant.**
(Raising his Sceptre) - But I testify, Fratres et Sorores, that our common heritage is life in the Holy Spirit. (He lowers his Sceptre.) Honourable Frater Hiereus, how many are the officers?

**Hiereus.**
These also are three - the Stolistes, the Dadouchos and the Kerux, besides the Sentinel, who stands armed on the further side of the Portal, who guards that side, receiving communications from without, admitting members and taking charge of the Candidate when he comes to the vestibule of the Holy Temple. (The Dadouchos, standing in his place, raised the Thurible, and as incense issues therefrom:)

Temple is guarded without: let the heart be guarded within. (A momentary pause.)

**Hierophant.**

Honourable Frater Hiereus, lift up the sword of judgment, and standing by the hither side of the Portal, assure yourself that all present have seen the Light in the East. (The Hiereus leaves his Throne, passes to the door of the Temple, where he draws his Sword and raises it.)

**Hiereus.**

Fratres et Sorores of the Holy Order of the Golden Dawn give the signs of a Seeker for the Light. (This is done accordingly, and the Hiereus sheathes his Sword. He gives the Signs of a Neophyte.)

**Hiereus.**

Truly Honoured Hierophant, the Orient from on High hath visited us. (The Signs are repeated by the Hierophant. The Hiereus returns to his place.)

**Hierophant.**

Those who are present among us are more especially the watchers from within. Stand about us in Thy Holy Place, O Lord, and keep us pure in Thy precincts. (This is said with raised eyes and uplifted Sceptre. There is a momentary pause.)

**Hierophant.**

Let the number of officers in this Grade and the symbolism of their offices be proclaimed once again, that the graces

**Hierophant.**

Fratres et Sorores of the Isis Urania Temple, duly assembled under warrant for the Mysteries of the Golden Dawn, assist me to open the Temple of our Holy Order in the Grade of Neophyte.

**Kerux.**
Hekas. Hekas, este bebeloi.

(He returns to his place by the South and West, giving the Signs of the Grades as he passes the Throne of the Hierophant. Except in the reverse circumambulation at the close of this Grade, the course of the sun must be followed in the movements of all Officers and Members. The salute of the Grade must be given when passing the Hierophant and on entering or leaving the Temple.)

**Hierophant.**

Frater Kerux, see that the Temple is guarded on the further side of the Portal, as an outward sign of the mysteries of prudence that are within. (The Kerux gives one knock on the hither side of the door. The Sentinel responds in the same manner on the outer side, using the hilt of his sword.)

**Kerux.**

(Raising his Wand) - Truly Honoured Hierophant, the Temple is guarded without, the door is secured within, and I stand on the hither side as the witness of vigilance and the gate of prudence.

**Hierophant.**

(With raised eyes and uplifted Sceptre). Fratres et Sorores, let us put away the thoughts of the outer world. The

## PRAYER BEFORE THE THRONE

**Hierophant.**
Creator of the Universe, Lord of the Visible Worlds. Who hast by Thy Supreme Power set up Thy Holy Signs in all the quarters of the Heavens and dost speak to us by day and by night in Thy greater and lesser luminaries. Thy suns and stars and constellations: Grant, we beseech Thee, that the hidden grace which abides in the Radiant East, the Dayspring of Light and the Font of Life, may in answer to this our prayer – be here and now communicated to the Throne of the Hierophant. Make him in Thy benignity the efficacious emblems of that Dawning Golden Light which illuminates the Path of Thy Mysteries, and may that light lead us to the attainment of the Quintessence, the tingeing Stone of the Wise, the Wisdom which has its source in Thee and the Beautitude which is found in Thy Presence.

(The Officers and the Temple are in this manner dedicated to the work about to be performed, and the clearing is done invariably with a solemn recollection of the intention belonging to its several points. If the Temple is opened to communicate a higher Grade than that of Neophyte, it must be preceded by this clearing in the same manner. In such case, the communication of the Neophyte Grade subsequently on the same day does not carry with it the necessity of another clearing. The Prayer being finished, the Hierophant takes his place on the Throne in the East, approaching it by the northern side of the pedestal before the Throne. He assumes his sceptre. Members are seated: a pause. All rise. The Sentinel leaves the Temple. The Kerux passes by the North-East side of the Temple, and so standing at the right hand but to the front of the Hierophant, and facing West, he raises his Lamp and Wand.)

the Pentagram in the South, carries Wand to the middle place and utters the Sacred Name:)

**Hierophant.**
ADNI. (He moves in the same manner to the West, performs the same working and utters the Sacred name:)

**Hierophant.**
EH-YEH. (He moves in the same manner to the North, performs the same working and utters the Sacred Word:)

**Hierophant.**
AGLA. (He returns in the same manner to the East, having thus circumambulated the Temple and traced a complete circle in the air with his Wand. This is the clearing of the Temple. Members face each quarter with Hierophant, who now faces East, extends his arms crosswise and says:)

**Hierophant.**
Before me RAPHAEL.
Behind me GABRIEL.
At my right hand MICHAEL.
At my left hand AURIEL.
For before me flames the Pentagram and behind me shines the Six-Rayed Star.

(This is the Angelical Formula, which brings the holy hills about the Jerusalem of the Temple and makes the Temple itself as a ring of holy hills about his own Jerusalem within. He finishes as he began, namely, with the SEALING PRAYER, which signifies the closing of the gates within and without against the images of evil. He goes before the Throne of the Hierophant, which he faces, and recites the following prayer.)

Temple or one of the Honourable Wardens proceeds to the clearing of the Temple as follows: With the first and second fingers and the thumb of his right hand he seals his forehead and says:)

**Hierophant.**
ATEH (He seals his breast and says:)

**Hierophant.**
MALKUTH. (He seals his right shoulder and says:)

**Hierophant.**
VE GEBURAH. (He seals his left shoulder and says:)

**Hierophant.**
VE GEDULAH. (He clasps his hands and says:)

**Hierophant.**
LE OLAHM. AMEN. (The operation hereof is more especially for his own cleansing, that he may be worthy to purify without. It is done facing the due East. All stand and turn eastward.)

## THE BANISHING

(He traces the Banishing Pentagram in the East with reversed Sceptre or Wand. He carries his Wand to the middle place of the Pentagram and pronounces slowly and distinctly the Sacred Name.)

**Hierophant.**
YOD, HE, VAU, HE. (He moves to the South, carrying the Wand upraised and pointed at the same angle. He traces

**5. The Frater Thurificans** wears a red surplice and a collar of green silk, from which depends a circular lamina, inscribed with an equilateral triangle, having the apex upward, as a symbol of Fire. He is in symbolical correspondence with the Master.

Certified a correct copy of the Autograph MS SACRAMENTUM REGIS, 5-6.

## THE HOLY ORDER OF THE GOLDEN DAWN
## THE SOLEMN CEREMONY OF
## OPENING THE TEMPLE IN THE LIGHT

(**The arrangement of the Temple is shown in the Official Diagram.**

**The Officers and Members being assembled within the door of the Sacred Precincts being closed and guarded by the Sentinel, who is seated with drawn sword on the hither side, the permanent Director of Ceremonies comes before the vacant Throne of the Hierophant, and says:**)

**Director of Ceremonies.**
Fratres et Sorores, the Lord is my light and my help. In the Name of Him Who rescues us from the darkness and the unredeemed places, and by command of the Honourable Wardens, I direct the Officers and Brethren to assume the clothing of their rank and Grades. Invest our portals, O Lord, and guard our thresholds. Do Thou clothe us in Thy grace and truth.

(The Members assume the insignia of their proper ribbons and collars. The Director of Ceremonies assists in the vesting of the Superior Officers. This being accomplished in solemn order and in the reverence of holy silence, the Hierophant of the having four circles at the end of the four arms and one circle toward the centre of the lowermost arm.

**2. The Honourable Frater Practicus** wears a yellow robe over his black habit, symbolising the beginning of transmutation in GOD. The symbol of the Eagle is embroidered thereon, upon the left side, with the inscription: FACIES QUARTA, FACIES AQUILAE. His collar is of violet silk, from which depends a circular lamina, inscribed with the letter HE, being the first HE of the Divine Name. He bears a Wand surmounted by a flaming heart.

**3. The Honourable Frater Theoreticus** wears a blue robe over his black habit, symbolising the aspiration and desire which initiate the great quest and reflect things unrealised. It bears the symbol of the Man embroidered thereon, upon the left side, with the inscription: FACIES SECUNDA, FACIES HOMINIS. His collar is of orange silk, from which depends a circular lamina, inscribed with the letter VAU. He bears a Wand, surmounted by an open eye, signifying the eye of mind.

**4. The Auxiliary Frater Zelator** wears a cloak of reddish brown, corresponding to the Adamic earth and symbolising the first movement of the Divine Spirit toward the making of a living soul. The symbol of the Ox is embroidered thereon, with the inscription: FACIES UNA, FACIES CHERUB. His collar is of blue-green silk, from which depends a circular lamina, inscribed with the letter HE, being the HE final of the Divine Name. He bears a Wand, surmounted by a Calvary Cross, having a crown upon the upper arms. The Frater Zelator is in symbolical correspondence with the Guide of the Paths and Grades.

3. THE HONOURABLE FRATER THEORETICS, id est, Mens Conscia Sponsi-Guide of the Paths and Grades.

4. THE AUXILIARY FRATER ZELATOR, id est, Terra Illuminata - Proclamator et Lucifer.

5. THE FRATER THURIFICANS, id est, Thuribulum Ferens - Thurifer.

6. THE FRATER AQUARIUS, id est, Aquam Benedictam Ferens - Aquarius.

7. THE FRATER OSTIARIUS, id est, Custos Liminis, A Novice of the Rosy Cross Guard.

8. The Imperator, or Chief of the Rite, presides ex officio in all Grades of the Fellowship, either personally or by his appointed Substitute.

In those cases where certain Offices are taken by Sorores of the Fellowship, the necessary alterations are made in the modes of address.

**THE CLOTHING OF
CELEBRANTS AND OFFICERS**

**1. The Honourable Frater Philosophicus** wears a green robe over his black habit and a collar of red silk, from which depends a circular lamina, inscribed with the letters YOD. The green colour of the Master's robe represents the growth in life which is of GOD. The symbol of the Lion is embroidered thereon, upon the left side, with the inscription: FACIES TERTIA, FACIES LEONIS. The Master bears a Wand, surmounted by a Calvary Cross, fifty years ago. This is a remarkable admission of the efficacy not merely of ritual per se, but of what I would otherwise have stamped as pompous, flatulent, turgid bible-thumping which I dislike heartily.

There are some magnificent lines in here. In the event that some of my readers may wish to institute a new Golden Dawn temple, many of these lines could well be incorporated into the ancient rituals.

In the event that some already initiated members of the Orders are desirous of so-called higher grades. Waite's Adeptus Major Ritual might provide some basic features which could be incorporated into what they know of the conventional Order Rituals.

## THE CEREMONY OF RECEPTION
## IN THE GRADE OF NEOPHYTE

**Newly constructed from the Cipher Manuscripts, and issued by the authority of the concealed superiors of the second order, to members of recognised temples. Certified in Conformity with the Secret Doctrine and Knowledge of the ROSY CROSS.**

**SACRAMENTUM REGIS,
KEEPER OF THE SACRED MYSTERY.**

### THE OFFICERS OF THE GRADE

1. THE HONOURABLE FRATER PHILOSOPHICUS, id est, Propositum Conscium Dei - Master of the Temple.

2. THE HONOURABLE FRATER PRACTICUS, id est, Desiderium Conscium Dei - Warden of the Temple.

## THE FELLOWSHIP OF THE ROSEY CROSS
### From The Complete Golden Dawn System of Magic
By Israel Regardie[1]
New Falcon Publications, First Edition 1984

At this juncture, I would like very much to present three rituals written by Arthur Edward Waite for his own Order which he called The Fellowship of the Rosy Cross. As might be expected the text is Christian and biblical. Waite was raised a Roman Catholic. It is also classical Waite in that he was compelled to insert quite frequently Latin phrases which, from the ritualistic viewpoint, is not a bad idea since a strange tongue may excite the inner sense of wonder and worship. In ritual it is excusable. In prose it is unforgivable - at least to the extent that it is used by Waite in his various writings.

It is also typical Waite in that it is ponderous, turgid and repetitive. I am no great advocate or admirer of Waite's literary output. He had so much to say in reality, but his literary style got in the way to obscure his message.

Yet, in these rituals of the Neophyte, Adeptus Minor and Major grades, given me through the courtesy of Robert W. Gilbert of Bristol who is writing a biography on Waite, I have found myself strangely moved. It is rather like being escorted through the Adeptus Minor ritual again, though this time to the tune of another melody, in the language of another day, in the spirit of another religion. In spite of my own resistance to Waite, I find myself choked a little, tearful of eye, exalted in spirit as I was

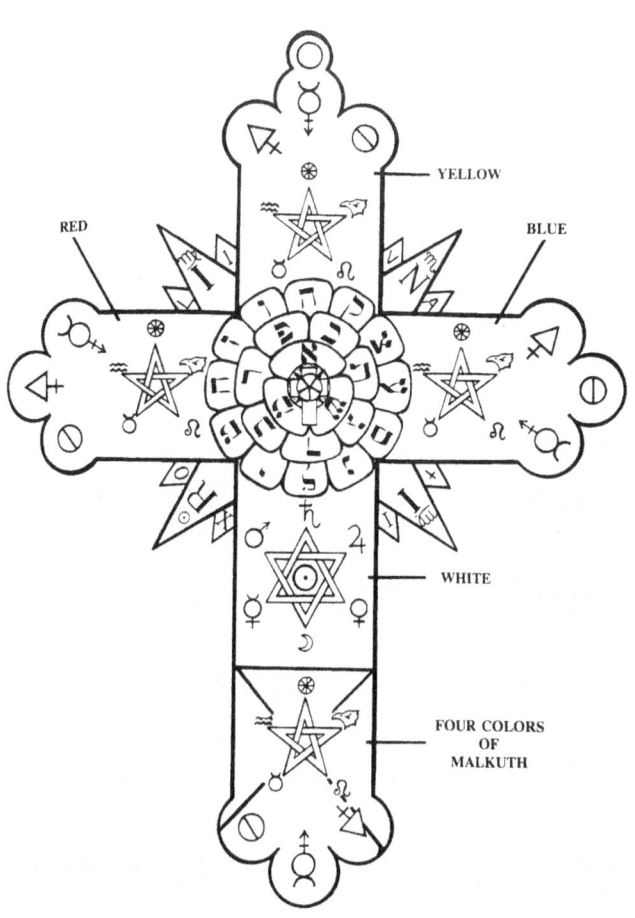

- YELLOW
- RED
- BLUE
- WHITE
- FOUR COLORS OF MALKUTH

## MOON IN CANCER, 20° - 30°.
## THE LORD OF BLENDED PLEASURE
## FOUR OF CUPS

Four cups, the two upper overflow into the two lower, which do not overflow. A hand grasps a bunch of lotuses from which ascends a stem bearing one flower at the top of the card, from which water issues into two top cups. From the centre two leaves pass right and left, making as it were a cross between the four cups. Luna and Cancer are above and below.

Success or pleasure approaching their end. A stationary period in happiness which may or may not continue. It does not show marriage and love so much as the previous symbol. It is too passive a symbol to represent perfectly complete happiness. Swiftness, hunting and pursuing. Acquisition by contention; injustice sometimes. Some drawbacks to pleasure implied.

Chesed of Heh. (Receiving pleasure, but some slight discomfort and anxieties, therewith. Blended pleasure and success.) Therein rule Hayayel and Mevamayah.

## VENUS IN CANCER, 1° - 10°. LORD OF LOVE
## TWO OF CUPS

Hand at lower part from cloud holds lotuses. A Lotus flower rises above water, which occupies the lowest part of card, and rises above the hand holding the Lotus. From this water-lily flower, from which a white water gushes like a fountain. Crossed on the stem just beneath are two Dolphins, Argent and Or, on to which the water falls and from which it pours in full streams, like jets of gold and silver, into two cups, which in their turn overflow, flooding the lower part of the card. Above and below Venus and Cancer.

Harmony of masculine and feminine united. Harmony, pleasure, mirth, subtlety, sometimes folly, dissipation, waste, and silly action, according to dignity.

Chokmah of Heh. (Marriage, home, pleasure.) Herein rule Ayoel and Chabooyah.

## MERCURY IN CANCER, 10° - 20°.
## LORD OF ABUNDANCE
## THREE OF CUPS

Hands as before holds group of Lotuses of Water-lilies, from which two flowers rise on either side of, and overhanging the top cup, pouring into it the white water. Flowers in the same way pour water into the lower cups. All the cups overflow, the topmost into the two others, and these upon the lower part of the card. Above and below Mercury and Cancer.

Abundance, plenty, success, pleasure, sensuality, passive success, good luck and fortune. Love, gladness, kindness and bounty. According to dignity.

Binah of Heh. (Plenty, hospitality, eating and drinking, pleasure, dancing, new clothes, merriment.) Herein rule Raphael and Yebomayah.

## MARS IN GEMINI, 10° - 20°.
## THE LORD OF DESPAIR AND CRUELTY
## NINE OF SWORDS

Four hands (somewhat as in preceding symbol) hold eight swords upright but with the points falling away from each other. A fifth hand holds a ninth sword upright in the centre, as if it had disunited them, and struck them asunder. No rose at all is shown (as if it were not merely cut in pieces but completely and definitely destroyed). Above and below Mars and Gemini.

Despair, cruelty, pitilessness, malice, suffering, want, loss, misery. Burden, oppression, patience, unselfishness, etc., according to dignity.

Yesod of Vau. Therein rule Aaneval and Mochayel.

## SUN IN GEMINI, 20° - 30°. LORD OF RUIN
## TEN OF SWORDS

Four hands (as in previous symbol) hold eight swords with points falling away from each other. Two hands hold two swords crossed in the centre (as if their junction had disunited the others). No rose, flower or bud is shown. Above and below are Sun and Gemini.

(Almost a worse symbol than Nine of Swords.) Undisciplined warring force, complete disruption and failure. Ruin of all plans and projects. Disdain, insolence and impertinence, yet mirth and jolly therewith. A Marplot, loving to overthrow the happiness of others, a repeater of things, given to much unprofitable speech, and on many words, yet clever, acute, and eloquent, etc., depending on dignity.

Mulkuth of Vav. (Ruin, death, defeat, disruption.) Herein rule Dambayah and Menqal.

Promises of success unfulfilled. (Shown in the symbolism of the rosebuds, which do not as it were come to anything.) Loss of apparently promising fortune. Hopes deceived and crushed. Disappointment. Misery, slavery, necessity and baseness. A cultivator of land, and yet is loser thereby. Sometimes it denotes slight and isolated gains with no fruits resulting therefrom, and of no further account, though seeming to promise well. According to dignity.

Netzach of Heh. (Unprofitable speculation and employment. Little gain for much labour.) Therein rule Herochiel and Mitzrael.

### JUPITER IN GEMINI, 1º - 10º.
### LORD OF SHORTENED FORCE
### EIGHT OF SWORDS

Four hands as usual, each holding two swords, points upwards, touching near top of card, two hands lower on left, two on right of card. The rose of other sword symbols re-established in centre. Above and below are Jupiter and Gemini.

Too much force applied to small things, too much attention to detail, at expense of principle and more important points. Ill-dignified, these qualities produce malice, pettiness, and domineering qualities.

Patience in detail of study, great ease in some things, counter-balanced by equal disorder in others. Impulsive, equally fond of giving or receiving money, or presents. Generous, clever, acute, selfish, and without strong feeling of affection. Admires wisdom, yet applies it to small and unworthy objects.

Hod Vav. (Narrow, restricted, petty, a prison.) Herein rule Vemibael and Yohohel.

Loss of money or position. Trouble about material things. Toil, labour, land cultivation, building, knowledge and acuteness of earthly things, poverty, carefulness. Kindness, sometimes money regained after severe toil and labour. Unimaginative, harsh, stern, determined, obstinate.

Geburah of Heh final. (Loss of profession, loss of money, monetary anxiety.) Therein rule Mibahiah and Pooyal.

### MOON IN TAURUS, 10° - 20°.
### LORD OF MATERIAL SUCCESS
### SIX OF PENTACLES

Hand holding a rose branch with white roses and buds, each of which touch a pentacle. Above and below Luna and Taurus represent the Decante.

Success and gain in material undertakings, power, influence, rank, nobility, rule over the people. Fortunate, successful, just and liberal. If ill-dignified, may be purse-proud, insolent from success, or prodigal.

Tiphareth of Heh final. (Success in material things. Prosperity in business.) Herein rule Nemamiah and Yeyelal.

### SATURN IN TAURUS, 20° - 30°.
### THE LORD OF SUCCESS UNFULFILLED
### SEVEN OF PENTACLES

Hand from a cloud holding rose branch of seven pentacles arranged as in Rubeus. No other buds shown, and five of which overhang but do not touch the five upper pentacles. No other buds shown, and none are near or touch the two lower pentacles. Above and below are Saturn and Taurus.

Established force and strength. Realisation of hope. Completion of labour, success of the struggle. Pride, nobility, wealth, power, conceit. Rude self assumption and insolence. Generosity, obstinacy according to dignity.

Binah of Yod. (Pride, arrogance and self-assertion.) Herein rule Hechashiah and Aamamiah.

### VENUS IN ARIES, 20° - 30°.
### LORD OF PERFECTED WORK
### FOUR OF WANDS

Two hand as before, issuing from clouds each side of card, and clasped in centre with First Order grip, holding four wands crossed. Flames issue at point of junction. Above and below are two small flaming wands with Venus and Aries, representing the Decan.

Perfection, a completion of a thing built up with trouble and labour. Rest after labour. Subtlety, cleverness, beauty, mirth, success in completion. Reasoning faculty, conclusion drawn from previous knowledge. Unreadiness, unreliable, and unsteady, through over anxiety and hurriedness of action. Graceful in manners. At times insincere, etc.

Chesod of Yod. (Settlement, arrangement, completion.) Herein rule Nanael and Nithal.

### MERCURY IN TAURUS, 1° - 10°.
### THE LORD OF MATERIAL TROUBLE
### FIVE OF PENTACLES

Hand holding a branch of White Rose Tree, from which roses are falling, leaving no buds behind. Five pentacles similar to Ace. Mercury and Taurus for Decan.

Happiness, yet almost more truly happy. Pleasure, dissipation, debauchery.

Pity, quietness, peacemaking, Kindness, generosity, wantonness, waste, etc., according to dignity.

Malkuth of Heh. (Matters definitely arranged as wished, complete good fortune.) Herein rule Aasliah and Mihal.

[This is not such a good card as stated above. It represents boredom and quarrelling arising therefrom: disgust springing from too great luxury. In particular it could represent drug habits, the sottish excess of pleasure and the revenge of nature.]

### MARS IN ARIES, 1° - 10°.
### THE LORD OF DOMINION
### TWO OF WANDS

Hand grasping two Wands crossed. Flames issue from the point of junction. On two small wands, above and below, with flames issuing from them, are Mars and Aries.

Strength, dominion, harmony of rule and justice. Boldness, courage, fierceness, shamelessness, revenge, resolution, generous, proud, sensitive, ambitious, refined, restless, turbulent, sagacious withal, yet unforgiving and obstinate, according to dignity.

Chokmah of Yod. (Influence over others. Authority, power, dominion.) Rule therein Vehooel and Deneyal.

### SUN IN ARIES, 10° - 20°.
### THE LORD OF ESTABLISHED STRENGTH
### THREE OF WANDS

Hand issuing from clouds holds three wands in centre. Two crossed and one upright. Flames from point of junction. Above and below are Sun and Aries.

Misery and repining without cause. Seeking after riches. Instability according to dignity.

Hod of Heh. (Success abandoned, decline of interest in anything.) Herein rule Vavaliah and Yelahiah.

## JUPITER IN PISCES, 10° - 20°.
## THE LORD OF MATERIAL HAPPINESS
## NINE OF CUPS

Hand from cloud holding Lotuses or water lilies, one flower of which overhangs each cup, and from which water pours. All the cups are full and running over. Above and below are the symbols of Jupiter and Pisces representing the Decan.

Complete and perfect realisation of pleasure and happiness almost perfect. Self-praise, vanity, conceit, much talking of self, yet kind and lovable, and may be self-denying therewith. Highminded, not easily satisfied with small and limited ideas. Apt to be maligned through too much self-assumption. A good, generous, but, maybe, foolish nature.

Yesod of Heh. (Complete success, pleasure, happiness, wish fulfilled.) Therein rule Saliah and Aariel.

## MARS IN PISCES, 20° - 30°.
## THE LORD OF PERFECTED SUCCESS
## TEN OF CUPS

Hand holding bunch of Lotuses or water-lilies whose flowers pour a pure white water into all the cups, which all run over. The top cup is held sideways by a hand and pours water into top left hand cup. A single lotus flower surmounts top cup and is the source of the water that fills it. Above and are below Mars and Pisces.

Permanent and lasting success, happiness because inspired from above. Not sensual as Nine of Cups, The Lord of Material

## MOON IN AQUARIUS, 20° - 30°.
## THE LORD OF UNSTABLE EFFORT
## SEVEN OF SWORDS

Two hands as before, each holding swords. A third hand holds a single sword in the centre. The points of all the swords do just touch one another, the central sword not altogether dividing them. The rose of the previous symbols of this suit is held by the hand which holds the central Sword, as if the Victory were at its disposal. Above and below Luna and Aquarius. (In the small cards, the Lunar Decans are always represented by a crescent on its back.)

Partial success, yielding when victory is within grasp, as if the last reserves of strength were used up. Inclination to lose when on the point of gaining though not continuing the effort. Love of abundance, fascinated by display, given to compliment, affronts and insolences, and to detect and spy on another. Inclined to betray confidences, not always intentional. Rather vacillating and unreliable, according to dignity as usual.

Netzach of Vav. (Journey by land, in character untrustworthy.) Herein rule Michael and Hanihel.

## SATURN IN PISCES, 1° - 10°.
## THE LORD OF ABANDONED SUCCESS
## EIGHT OF SWORDS

A hand holding a group of stems of Lotuses or water lilies. There are only two flowers shown which bend over the two center cups pouring into them a white water. The cups are not yet filled. The three upper cups are empty. At top and bottom are Saturn and Pisces.

Temporary success, but without further result. Things thrown aside as soon as gained. Not lasting even in the matter in hand. Indolence in success. Journeying from place to place.

## VENUS IN AQUARIUS, 1° - 10°.
## THE LORD OF DEFEAT
## FIVE OF SWORDS

Two rayed hands each holding two swords nearly upright, but falling apart from each other, right and left of card. A third hand holds a sword upright in centre as if it had separated them. The petals of the rose (which in the four of Swords had been reinstated in the centre) are torn asunder and falling. Above and below the symbols of Venus and Aquarius.

Contest finished, and decided against the person, failure, defeat, anxiety, trouble, poverty, avarice, grieving after gain, laborious, unresting, loss and vileness of nature. Malicious, slandering, lying, spiteful and talebearing. A busybody and separator of friends, hating to see peace and love between others. Cruel yet cowardly, thankless, and unreliable. Clever and quick in thought and speech. Feelings of pity easily roused but unending. As dignity.

Geburah of Vav. (Defeat, loss, malice, spite, slander, evilspeaking.) Herein rule Aniel and Chaamiah.

## MERCURY IN AQUARIUS, 10° - 20°.
## THE LORD OF EARNED SUCCESS
## SIX OF SWORDS

Two hands as before, each holding three swords which cross in centre. Rose re-established hereon. Mercury and Aquarius above and below, supported on the points of two short daggers or swords.

Success after anxiety and trouble. Selfishness, beauty, conceit, but sometimes modesty therewith, dominion, patience, labour, etc., according to dignity.

Tiphareth of Vav. (Labour, work, journey by water.) Herein rule Rehaayal and Yeyeziel.

Chokmah of Heh final. (Pleasant change, visit to friends.) Herein rule Lekabel and Veshiriah.

## MARS IN CAPRICORN, 10° - 20°.
## THE LORD OF MATERIAL WORKS
## THREE OF PENTACLES

A white rayed Angelic hand as before, holding a branch of a Rose-tree, of which two white rose-buds touch and surmount the topmost pentacle. The latter are arranged in a Triangle.

Above and below are symbols of Mars and Capricorn. Working and constructive force, building up, erection, creation, realisation, and increase of material things, gain in commercial transactions, rank, increase of substance, influence, cleverness in business, selfishness, commencement of matter to be established later. Narrow and prejudiced, keen in matter of gain. Modified by dignity. Sometimes given to seeking after the impossible.

Binah of Heh final. (Business, paid employment, commercial transactions.) Therein rule Yechavah and Lehachiah.

## SUN IN CAPRICORN, 20° - 30°.
## THE LORD OF EARTHLY POWER
## FOUR OF PENTACLES

A hand holding a branch of a Rose-tree, but without flowers or buds, save that in the centre is one fully blown white rose. Four pentacles with Sun and Capricorn above and below. Assured material gain, success, rank, dominion, earthly power completed, but leading to nothing beyond. Prejudiced, covetous, suspicious, careful and orderly, but discontented.

Little enterprise or originality. Altered by dignity as usual. Chesed of Heh final. (Gain of money or influence. A present.) Therein rule Kevequiah and Mendial.

## SATURN IN SAGITTARIUS, 20° - 30°.
## THE LORD OF OPPRESSION
## TEN OF WANDS

Four hands upholding 8 wands crossed as before. A fifth hand at foot of card holding two wands upright which traverse the junction of the others. Above and below the symbols Saturn and Sagittarius. Flames issue therefrom.

Cruel and overbearing force and energy, but applied only to selfish and material ends. Sometimes shows failure in a matter, and the opposition too strong to be controlled arising from the person's too great selfishness at the beginning. Ill-will, levity, lying, malice, slander, envy, obstinacy, swiftness in evil, if ill-dignified. Also generosity, self-sacrifice, and disinterestedness when well-dignified.

Malkuth of Yod. (Cruelty, malice, revenge and injustice.) Therein rule Reyayel and Avamel.

## JUPITER IN CAPRICORN, 1° - 10°.
## LORD OF HARMONIOUS CHANGE
## TWO OF PENTACLES

Two wheels, discs or Pentacles similar to that of the Ace. They are united by a green and gold Serpent, bound about them like a figure of Eight. It holds its tail in its mouth. A white radiant Angelic hand grasps the centre or holds the whole. No roses enter into this card. Above and below are the symbols Jupiter and Capricorn. It is a revolving symbol.

The harmony of change. Alternation of gain and loss, weakness and strength, ever varying occupation, wandering, discounted with any fixed condition of things; now elated, now melancholy, industrious yet unreliable, fortunate through prudence of management, yet sometimes unaccountably foolish. Alternately talkative and suspicious. Kind yet wavering and inconsistent. Fortunate in journeying. Argumentative.

## MERCURY IN SAGITTARIUS, 1° - 10°.
## LORD OF SWIFTNESS
## EIGHT OF WANDS

Four white Angelic Hands radiating (two proceeding from each side) from clouds, clasped in two pairs in the centre with the grip of First Order. (see description above.) They hold 8 wands with flames issuing down them. Placed in the centre at top and bottom of card are the symbols of Mercury and Sagittarius, representing the Decan.

Too much force applied too suddenly. Very rapid rush, but too quickly passed and expended. Violent but not lasting. Swiftness. Rapidity. Courage, boldness, confidence, freedom, warfare. Violence, love of open air, field sports, garden, meadows. Generous, subtle, eloquent, yet somewhat untrustworthy. Rapacious, insolent, oppressive. Theft and robbery, according to dignity.

Hod of Yod. (Hasty communication and messages. Swiftness.) Therein rule Nithahiah and Haayah.

## MOON IN SAGITTARIUS, 10° - 20°.
## THE LORD OF GREAT STRENGTH
## NINE OF WANDS

Four Hands as in the previous symbol holding eight wands crossed four and four, but a fifth hand at the foot of the card holds another wand upright, which traverses the point of junction with the others. Flames leap therefrom. Above and below the symbols Luna (depicted horizontally) and Sagittarius.

Tremendous and steady force that cannot be shaken. Herculean strength, yet sometimes scientifically applied. Great success, but with strife and energy. Victory preceded by apprehension and fear. Health good and recovery, yet doubt. Generous, questioning and curious, fond of external appearances, intractable, obstinate.

Yesod of Yod. (Strength, power, health. Recovery from sickness.) Herein rule Yirthiel and Sahiah.

## SUN IN SCORPIO, 10° - 20°. LORD OF PLEASURE
## SIX OF CUPS

An Angelic hand as before, holds a group of stems of Lotuses or water lilies from which six flowers bend, one over each cup. From these flowers a white glistening water flows into the cup as from a fountain, but they are not yet full. Above and below are the symbols of Sun and Scorpio, representing the Decanate.

Commencement of steady increase, gain and pleasure, but commencement only. Also affront, detection, knowledge, and in some instances, contention and strife, arising from unwarranted self-assertion and vanity. Sometimes thankless and presumptuous. Sometimes amiable and patient, according to dignity.

Tiphareth of Heh. (Beginning of wish, happiness, success or enjoyment.) Therein rule Nelokhiel and Yeyayel.

## VENUS IN SCORPIO, 20° - 30°.
## LORD OF ILLUSIONARY SUCCESS
## SEVEN OF CUPS

A hand as usual holds the lotus stems which arise from the central lower cup. The hand is above this cup and below the middle one. With the exception of the central lower cup, each is overhung by a lotus flower, but no water falls from them into cups which are quite empty. Above and below are the symbols of the decanate, Venus and Scorpio.

Possibly victory, but neutralized by the supineness of the person. Illusionary success. Deception in the moment of apparent victory. Lying, error, promises unfulfilled. Drunkenness, wrath, vanity, lust, fornication, violence against women. Selfish dissipation. Deception in love and friendship. Often success gained, but not followed up. Modified by dignity.

Netzach of Heh. (Lying. Promises unfulfilled. Error. Deception, slight success at outset, but want of energy to retain it.) Therein rule Melchel and Chahaviah.

## JUPITER IN LIBRA, 20° - 30°.
## THE LORD OF REST FROM STRIFE
## FOUR OF SWORDS

Two white Angelic radiating hands, each holding two swords, which four cross in the centre. The rose of five petals with white radiations is reinstated on the point of intersection. Above and below, on the points of two small daggers are the symbols of Jupiter and Libra representing the Decan.

Rest from sorrow, yet after and through it. Peace from and after war. Relaxation of anxiety. Quietness, rest, ease and plenty, yet after struggle. Goods of this life, abundance. Modified by the dignity as in the other cases.

Chesed of Vav. (Convalescence, recovery from sickness, change for the better.) Herein rule Laviah and Kelial.

## MARS IN SCORPIO, 1° - 10°.
## LORD OF LOSS IN PLEASURE
## FIVE OF CUPS

A white radiating Angelic hand as before holding Lotuses or water lilies of which the flowers are falling right and left. Leaves only and no buds surmount them. These lotus stems ascend between the cups in the manner of a fountain, but no water flows therefrom, neither is there water in any of the Cups, which are somewhat of the shape of the magical implement of the Z.A.M. Above and below are the symbols of Mars and Scorpio, representing the Decan.

Death or end of pleasures: disappointment, sorrow and loss in those things from which pleasure is expected. Sadness, deceit, treachery, ill-will, detraction, charity and kindness ill-requited. All kinds of anxieties and troubles from unexpected and unsuspected sources.

Geburah of Heh. (Disappointments in love, marriage broken off, unkindness from a friend, loss of friendship.) Therein rule Livoyah and Pehilyah.

Contradictory characteristics in the same nature. Strength through suffering. Pleasure after Pain. Sacrifice and trouble yet strength arising therefrom symbolised by the position of the rose, as though the pain itself had brought forth beauty. Peace restored, truce, arrangement of differences, justice. Truth and untruth. Sorrow and sympathy for those in trouble, aid to the weak and oppressed, unselfishness. Also an inclination to repetition of affronts if once pardoned, of asking questions of little moment, want of tact, often doing injury when meaning well. Talkative.

Chokmah of Vav. (Quarrels made up, but still some tension in relationships. Actions sometimes selfish and sometimes unselfish.) Herein rule the great Angels Yezalel and Mabahel.

## SATURN IN LIBRA, 10° - 20°. LORD OF SORROW
## THREE OF SWORDS

Three white radiating Angelic hands issuing from clouds and holding three swords upright (as if the central sword had struck apart from the two others which were crossed in the preceding symbol.) The central sword cuts asunder the Rose of Five Petals (which in the preceding symbol grew at the junction of the swords). Its petals are falling, and no white rays issue from it. Above and below the central Sword are the symbols of Saturn and Libra, referring to the Decanate.

Disruption, interruption, separation, quarrelling, sowing of discord and strife, mischief-making, sorrow, tears, yet mirth in evil pleasures, singing, faithfulness in promises, honesty in money transactions, selfish and dissipated, yet sometimes generous, deceitful in words and repetition. The whole according to dignity.

Binah of Vau. (Unhappiness, sorrow, tears.) Therein rule the Angels Harayel and Hoqmiah.

There are more buds arranged on the branches as well as flowers. Venus and Virgo above and below.

Complete realisation of material gain, inheritance, covetousness, treasuring of goods and sometimes theft, and knavery. All according to dignity.

Yesod of Heh. (Inheritance, much increase of goods.) Herein rule the mighty angels Hazayel and Aldiah.

### MERCURY IN VIRGO, 20° - 30°. LORD OF WEALTH
### TEN OF PENTACLES

An Angelic hand holding a branch by the lower extremity, whose roses touch all the pentacles. No buds however are shown. The symbols of Mercury and Virgo are above and below Pentacles.

Completion of material gain and fortune, but nothing beyond, as it were, at the very pinnacle of success. Old age, slothfulness, great wealth, yet sometimes loss in part, and later heaviness, dullness of mind, yet clever and prosperous in money transactions.

Malkuth of Heh. (Riches and wealth.) Herein rule the Angels Hihaayah and Laviah.

### MOON IN LIBRA, 1° - 10°.
### LORD OF PEACE RESTORED
### TWO OF SWORDS

Two crossed swords, like the air dagger of Z.A.M., each held by a white radiating Angelic hand. Upon the point where the two cross is a rose of five petals, emitting white Rays, and top and bottom of card are two small daggers, supporting respectively the symbols of Luna (in horizontal position) and Libra, representing the Decan.

Possible victory, depending upon the energy and courage exercised; valour, opposition, obstacles, difficulties, yet courage to meet them, quarrelling, ignorance, pretence, wrangling and threatening, also victory in small and unimportant things, and influence over subordinates. Depending on dignity as usual.

Netzach of Yod. (Opposition yet courage.) Herein rule the two great Angels Mahashiah and Lelahel.

## SUN IN VIRGO, 1° - 10°. LORD OF PRUDENCE
## EIGHT OF PENTACLES

A white radiating Angelic hand issuing from a cloud and grasping a branch of a Rose tree, with four white roses thereon which touch only the four lowermost pentacles. No rosebuds seen, but only leaves touch the four uppermost disks. All the Pentacles are similar Geomantic figure Populus.

Above and below them are the symbols Sol and Virgo for the Decan. Over-careful in small things at the expense of the great. "Penny-wise and pound-foolish." Gain of ready money in small sums. Mean, avariciousness. Industrious, cultivation of land, hoarding, lacking in enterprise.

Hod of Heh. (Skill, prudence, cunning.) Here rule those mighty angels Akaiah and Kehethel.

## VENUS IN VIRGO, 10° - 20°.
## LORD OF MATERIAL GAIN
## NINE OF PENTACLES

A white radiating Angelic hand as before holding a Rose branch with nine white roses, each of which touches a Pentacle. (See the Golden Dawn Tarot Deck by Wang and Regardie, U.S. Game Systems, 1978-9 for the various arrangements indicated in these descriptions.)

Violent strife and contest, boldness, rashness, cruelty, violence, lust and desire, prodigality and generosity, depending on well or ill dignified.

Geburah of Yog. (Quarrelling and fighting.) This decan hath its beginning from the Royal Star of Leo, and unto it are allotted the two Great Angels of the Schemhamephoresch Vahaviah and Yelayel.

## JUPITER IN LEO, 10° - 20°, THE LORD OF VICTORY
## SIX OF WANDS

Two hands in grip, as in the last, holding six Wands crossed, 3 and 3. Flames issuing from the point of junction. Above and below are two short wands with flames issuing from a cloud at the lower part of the card, surmounted respectively by the symbols of Jupiter and Leo, representing the Decanate.

Victory after strife, success through energy and industry, love, pleasure gained by labour, carefulness, sociability and avoiding of strife, yet victory therein. Also insolence, pride of riches and success, etc. The whole depending on dignity.

Tiphareth of Yod. (Gain.) Hereunto are allotted the Great Angels from the Schemhamephoresch, Saitel and Olmiah.

## MARS IN LEO, 20° - 30°, THE LORD OF VALOUR
## SEVEN OF WANDS

Two hands holding by grip, as before, 6 Wands, three crossed by three, a third hand issuing from a cloud at the lower part of the card holding an upright wand, which passes between the others. Flames leap from the point of junction. Above and below the central wand are the symbols Mars and Leo, representing the Decan.

## HOD

The Four Eights. Generally show solitary success; i.e., success in the matter for the time being, but not leading to much result apart from the thing itself.

## YESOD

The Four Nines. Generally they show very great fundamental force. Executive power, because they rest on firm basis, powerful for good or evil.

## MALKUTH

The Four Tens. Generally show fixed culminated completed Force, whether good or evil. The matter thoroughly and definitely determined. Similar to the force of the Nines, but ultimating it, and carrying it out. These are the meanings in the most general sense.

Here follow the more particular descriptions and meanings. **Decan cards are always modified by the other symbols with which they are in contact.**

## SATURN IN LEO, 1° - 10°. THE LORD OF STRIFE
## FIVE OF WANDS

Two white radiant angelic hands issuing from clouds right and left of the centre of the card. They are clasped together as in the grip of the First Order, i.e. the four fingers of each right crooked into each other, the thumbs meeting above; and they hold at the same time by their centres Five Wands, or torches, which are similar to the wand of a Z.A.M. Four Wands cross each other, but the Fifth is upright in the centre. Flames leap from the point of junction. Above the central Wand is the symbol Saturn and below it that of Leo representing the Decanate.

## CHOKMAH

The Four Twos symbolise the Powers of the King and Queen; first uniting and initiating the Force, but before the Knight and Knave are thoroughly brought into action. Therefore do they generally imply the initiation and fecundation of a thing.

## BINAH

The Four Threes, generally, represent the realisation of action owing to the Prince being produced. The central symbol on each card. Action definitely commenced for good or evil.

## CHESED

The Four Fours. Perfection, realisation, completion, making a matter settled and fixed.

## GEBURAH

The Four Fives. Opposition, strife and struggle; war, obstacle to the thing in hand. Ultimate success or failure is otherwise shown.

## TIPHARETH

The Four Sixes. Definite accomplishment, and carrying out a matter.

## NETZACH

The Four Sevens. Generally shows a force, transcending the material plane, and is like unto a crown which is indeed powerful but requireth one capable of wearing it. The sevens then show a possible result which is dependent on the action then taken. They depend much on the symbols that accompany them.

## THE THIRTY-SIX DECANS

Here follow the descriptions of the smaller cards of the 4 Suits, thirty-six in number, answering unto the 36 Decans of the Zodiac. Commencing from the sign Aries, the Central Decans of each sign follow the order of the Days of the Week.

| Card | Decan | Meaning | Day |
|---|---|---|---|
| 3W | Aries | Established Strength | Sunday |
| 6P | Taurus | Material Success | Monday |
| 9S | Gemini | Despair and Cruelty | Tuesday |
| 3C | Cancer | Abundance | Wednesday |
| 6W | Leo | Victory | Thursday |
| 9P | Virgo | Material Gain | Friday |
| 3S | Libra | Sorrow | Saturday |
| 6C | Scorpio | Pleasure | Sunday |
| 9W | Sagittarius | Great Strength | Monday |
| 3P | Capricorn | Material Works | Tuesday |
| 6S | Aquarius | Earned Success | Wednesday |
| 9C | Pisces | Material Happiness | Thursday |

There being 36 Decanates and only seven Planets, it follows that one of the latter must rule over one more decanate than the others. This is the Planet Mars which is allotted the last decan of Pisces and first of Aries, because the long cold of the winter requires a great energy to overcome it and initiate spring.

The beginning of the decanates is from the Royal King Star of the Heart of the Lion, the great star Cor Leonis, and therefore is the first decanate that of Saturn in Leo.

Here follow the general meanings of the small cards of the Suits, as classified under the Nine Sephiroth below Kether.

## PRINCE OF THE CHARIOT OF EARTH
## KNIGHT OF PENTACLES

A winged kingly figure seated in a chariot drawn by a bull. He bears as a crest the symbol of the head of a winged bull. Beneath the chariot is land with many flowers. In one hand he bears on orb of gold held downwards, and in the other a sceptre surmounted by an Orb and cross.

Increase of matter, increase of good and evil, solidifies, practically applies things, steady, reliable. If ill-dignified, animal, material, stupid. Is either slow to anger, but furious if roused. Rules from 20° Aries to 20° of Taurus. Air of Earth, Prince and Emperor of the Gnomes.

## PRINCESS OF THE ECHOING HILLS
## ROSE OF THE PALACE OF EARTH
## KNAVE OF PENTACLES

A strong and beautiful Amazon figure with red brown hair, standing on grass and flowers. A grove of trees near her. Her form suggests Hera, Ceres, and Proserpine. She bears a winged ram's head as a crest, and wears a mantle of sheep's skin. In one hand she carries a sceptre with a circular disc, in the other a Pentacle similar to that of the Ace of Pentacles.

She is generous, kind, diligent, benevolent, careful, courageous, preserving, pitiful. Of ill-dignified, she is wasteful and prodigal. Rules over one Quadrant of the Heavens around the North Pole of the Ecliptic. Earth of Earth. Princess and Empress of the Gnomes. Throne of the Ace of Pentacles.

## PENTACLES

### LORD OF THE WILD AND FERTILE LAND
### KING OF THE SPIRIT OF EARTH
### KING OF PENTACLES

A dark winged Warrior with winged and crowned helmet; mounted on a light brown horse. Equipment as of the King of Wands. The winged head of a stag or antelope as a crest. Beneath the horse's feet is fertile land, with ripened corn. In one hand he bears a sceptre surmounted with a hexagram, in the other a pentacle like a Z.A.M.'s.

Unless very well dignified, he is heavy, dull, and material. Laborious, clever and patient in material matters. If ill-dignified he is avaricious, grasping, dull, jealous, not very courageous, unless assisted by other symbols. Rules from above 20° of Leo to 20° of Virgo. Fire of Earth. King of the Gnomes.

### QUEEN OF THE THRONES OF EARTH
### QUEEN OF PENTACLES

A woman of beautiful face with dark hair, seated upon a throne, beneath which is dark sandy earth. One side of her face is dark, the other light, and her symbolism is best represented in profile. Her attire is similar to that of the Queen of Wands. But she bears a sceptre surmounted by a cube, and in the other an Orb of gold.

She is impetuous, kind, timid, rather charming, greathearted, intelligent, melancholy, truthful, yet of many moods. Ill-dignified she is undecided, capacious, foolish, changeable. Rules from 20° Sagittarius to 20° Capricorn. Water of Earth. Queen of Gnomes.

hair long and waving in serpentine whirls, and whorl figures compose the scales of his armour. A drawn sword in one hand, a sickle in the other. With the sword he rules, with the sickle he slays.

Full of ideas and thoughts and designs, distrustful, suspicious, firm in friendship and enmity, careful, slow, overcautious. Symbolises Alpha and Omega, the Giver of Death, who slays as fast as he creates. Ill-dignified harsh, malicious, plotting, obstinate, yet hesitating and unreliable. Ruler from 20° Aquarius, Air of Air. Prince and Emperor of Sylphs and Sylphides.

## PRINCESS OF THE RUSHING WINDS
## LOTUS OF THE PALACE OF THE AIR
## KNAVE OF SWORDS

An Amazon figure with waving hair, slighter than the Rose of the Palace of Fire, Knave of Wands. Her attire is similar. The feet seem springy, giving the idea of swiftness. Weight changing from one foot to another, and body swinging round. She resembles a mixture of Minerva and Diana, her mantle resembles the Aegis of Minerva. She wears as a crest the head of Medusa with Serpent hair. She holds a sword in one hand and the other rests upon a small silver altar with grey smoke (no fire) ascending from it. Beneath her feet are white cirrous clouds.

Wisdom, strength, acuteness, subtleness in material things, grace and dexterity. If ill-dignified, she is frivolous and cunning. She rules a quadrant of the Heavens around Kether.

Earth of Air. Princess and Empress of the Sylphs and Sylphides. Throne of the Ace of Swords.

unless well-dignified. Ill-dignified, deceitful, tyrannical and crafty. Rules from 20° Taurus to 20° Gemini. Fire of Air. King of Sylphs and Sylphides.

## QUEEN OF THE THRONES OF AIR
## QUEEN OF SWORDS

A graceful woman with curly waving hair, like a Queen seated upon a Throne, and crowned. Beneath the Thrones are grey cumulous clouds. Her general attire is similar to that of the Queen of Wands. But she wears as a crest a winged child's head (like the head of an infantile Kerub seen sculptored on tombs.)

A drawn sword in one hand, and in the other a large bearded newly-severed head of a man.

Intensely perceptive, keen observation, subtle, quick, confident, often perseveringly accurate in superficial things, graceful, fond of dancing and balancing. Ill-dignified, cruel, Water of Air. Queen of the Sylphs and Sylphides.

## PRINCE OF THE CHARIOTS OF THE WINDS
## KNIGHTS OF SWORDS

A Winged Knight with a winged Crown, seated in a chariot drawn by Arch Fays, archons, or Arch Fairies, represented as winged youths very slightly draped, with butterfly wings, heads encircled with a fillet with Pentagrams thereon, and holding wands surmounted by Pentagram shaped stars. The same butterfly wings are on their feet and fillet. General equipment is that of the Knight of Wands, but he bears as a crest, as winged Angelic Head, with a Pentagram on the Brow. Beneath the chariot are grey rain clouds or nimbi. His

## PRINCESS OF THE WATERS AND
## LOTUS OF THE PALACE OF THE FLOODS
## KNAVE OF CUPS

A beautiful Amazon-like figure, softer in nature than the Princess of Wands. Her attire is similar. She stands on a sea with foaming spray. Away to her right is a Dolphin. She wears as a crest on her Helmet, belt and buskins, a Swan with opening wings. She bears in one hand a Lotus, and in the other an open Cup from which a Turtle issues. Her mantle is lined with swans-down, and is thin floating material.

Sweetness, poetry, gentleness, and kindness. Imagination, dreamy, at times indolent, yet courageous if roused. Ill-dignified she is selfish and luxurious. She rules a quadrant of the Heavens around Kether. Earth of Water. Princess and Empress of Nymphs and Undines. Throne of the Ace of Cups.

## SWORDS

## LORD OF THE WINDS AND BREEZES
## KING OF THE SPIRIT OF AIR
## KING OF SWORDS

A winged Warrior with crowned and winged Helmet, mounted upon a brown steed, his general equipment is as that of the King of Wands, but he wears as a crest a winged six-pointed star, similar to those represented on the heads of Castor and Pollux, the Dioscuri, the Twins Gemini (a part of which constellation is included in his rule). He holds a drawn sword with the Sigil of his Scale upon its pommel. Beneath his horse's feet are dark, driving, stratus clouds.

He is active, clever, subtle, fierce, delicate, courageous, skillful, but inclined to domineer. Also overvalue small things,

## QUEEN OF THE THRONES OF THE WATERS
## QUEEN OF CUPS

A very beautiful fair woman like a crowned Queen, seated upon a Throne, beneath which is flowing water, wherein Lotuses are seen. Her general dress is similar to that of the Queen of Wands, but upon her Crown, cuirass and buskins is seen an ibis with opened wings, and beside her is the same Bird, whereon her hand rests. She holds a Cup, wherefrom a crayfish issues. Her face is dreamy. She holds a Lotus in the other hand upon the ibis.

She is imaginative, poetic, kind, yet not willing to take much trouble for another, coquettish, good-natured, underneath a dreamy appearance. Imagination stronger than feeling. Very much affected by other influences, and therefore more dependent upon good or ill-dignity than upon most other symbols. She rules from 20° Gemini to 20° Cancer. Water of Water. Queen of Nymphs and Undines.

## PRINCE OF THE CHARIOT OF THE WATERS
## KNIGHT OF CUPS

A winged Kingly figure with a winged crown, seated in a chariot drawn by an Eagle. On the wheel is the symbol of a Scorpion. The Eagle is borne as a crest upon his crown, cuirass and buskins. General attire like Knight of Wands. Beneath his chariot is the calm and stagnant water of a lake. His scale armour resembles feathers more than scales. He holds in one hand a Lotus, and the other a Cup, charged with the sigil of his Scale. A serpent issues from his Cup, and has its head tending down to the waters of the Lake.

He is subtle, violent, crafty and artistic. A fierce nature with calm exterior. Powerful for good or evil, but more attracted to evil, if allied with apparent Power or Wisdom. If ill-dignified he is intensely evil and merciless. He rules from 20° of Libra to 20° Scorpio. Air of Water. Prince and Emperor of Nymphs and Undines.

A mantel lined with tiger's skin falls back from her shoulders. Her right hand rests on a small golden or brazen Altar, ornamented with Ram's heads, and with Flames of Fire leaping from it. Her left hand leans on a long and heavy club, swelling at the lower end, where the sigil is placed. It has Flames of Fire leaping from it the whole way down, but the flames are ascending. This Club or torch is much longer than that carried by the King or Queen. Beneath her firmly placed feet are leaping Flames of Fire.

Brilliance, courage, beauty, force, sudden in anger or love, desire of power, enthusiasms, revenge.

Ill-dignified, superficial, theatrical, cruel, unstable, domineering. She rules the heavens over one quadrant of the portion round the North Pole. Earth of Fire. Princess and Empress of the Salamanders. Throne of the Ace of Wands.

## CUPS

## LORD OF THE WAVES AND THE WATERS
## KING OF CUPS

A beautiful youthful winged Warrior, with flying hair, riding upon a white horse, which latter is not winged. His general equipment is similar to that of the King of Wands, but upon his helmet, cuirass and bushkins is a peacock with opened wings. He holds a Cup in his hand, bearing the sigil of the Scale. Beneath his horses' feet is the sea. From the cup issues a crab.

Graceful, poetic, venusian, indolent, but enthusiastic if roused. Ill-dignified, he is sensual, idle, and untruthful. He rules the heavens from above 29° of Aquarius to 20° Pisces including the greater part of Pegasus. Fire of Water. King of Undines and of Nymphs.

## THE PRINCE OF THE CHARIOT OF FIRE
## KNIGHT OF WANDS

A Kingly figure (but **not** a King) with a golden winged Crown, seated on a Chariot. He has large white wings. One wheel of his Chariot is shewn. He wears corselet and buskin of scale armour, decorating with winged Lions' heads, which symbol also surmounts his crown. His chariot is drawn by a lion. His arms are bare, save for the shoulder pieces of the corselet, and he bears a torch or firewand, somewhat similar to that of the Z.A.M. Beneath the Chariot are flames, some waved, some salient.

Swift, strong, hasty, rather violent, yet just and generous, noble and scorning meanness. If ill-dignified, cruel, intolerant, prejudiced, and ill-natured. He rules the Heavens from above the last decan of Cancer to the 2nd decan of Leo. Hence he includes most of Leo Minor. Air of Fire. Prince and Emperor of Salamanders.

## PRINCESS OF THE SHINING FLAME–
## THE ROSE OF THE PALACE OF FIRE
## KNAVE OF WANDS

A very strong and beautiful woman, with flowing red-golden hair, attired like an Amazon. Her shoulders, arms, bosom and knees are bare. She wears a short kilt, reaching to the knees. Round her waist is a broad belt of scale mail, narrow at the side, broad in the front and back, and having a winged tiger's head in front. She wears a Corinthian shaped helmet, and Crown with a long plume. It also is surmounted by a tiger's head, and the same symbol forms the buckle of her scale-mail buskins.

Beneath the rushing feet of his steed are waving flames of Fire. He is active, generous, fierce, sudden and impetuous. If ill-dignified he is evil-minded, cruel, bigoted, brutal. He rules the celestial Heavens from above the 20th degree of Scorpio to the first two Decans of Sagittarius and this includes a part of the constellation Hercules (who also carries a club). Fire of Fire. King of the Salamanders.

## QUEEN OF THE THRONES OF FLAME
## QUEEN OF WANDS

A crowned Queen with long red-golden hair, seated upon a Throne, with steady Flames beneath. She wears a corselet and buskins of scale mail, revealed by her robe. Her arms are almost bare. On the cuirass and buskins are leopards' heads winged. The same symbol surmounteth her crown. At her side is a couchant Leopard on which her hands rest. She bears a long Wand with a very heavy conical head. The face is beautiful and resolute.

Adaptability, steady force applied to an object. Steady rule; great attractive power, power of command, yet liked notwithstanding. Kind and generous when not opposed. If ill-dignified, obstinate, revengeful, domineering, tyrannical and apt to turn suddenly against another without a cause. She rules the Heavens from above the last Decan of Pisces to above the twentieth degree of Aries, including a part above the last Decan of Pisces to above the twentieth degree of Aries, including a part of Andromeda. Water of Fire. Queen of the Salamanders or Salamandrines.

standing firmly by itself, only partially draped and having but little armour. Yet her power existeth not save by reason of the others, and then indeed it is mighty and terrible materially, and is the Throne of the forces of the Spirit. Woe unto whomsoever shall make war upon her when thus established!

## WHERE THE COURT CARDS OPERATE

The Princesses rule over the Four Parts of the Celestial Heavens which lie around the North Pole, and above the respective Kerubic Signs and the Zodiac, and they form the Thrones of the Powers of the Four Aces.

The Twelve Cards, 4 Kings, 4 Queens, and 4 Knights rule the Dominions of the Celestial Heavens between the realm of the Four Princesses and the Zodiac, as is hereafter shewn. And they, as it were, link together the signs.

## WANDS

## THE LORD OF THE FLAME AND THE LIGHTNING KING OF THE SPIRITS OF FIRE

### KING OF WANDS

A winged Warrior riding upon a black horse with flaming mane and tail. The horse itself is not winged. The Rider wears a winged Helmet (like an old Scandinavian and Gaulish Helmet) with a royal Crown. A corselet of scale-mail and buskins of the same, and a flowing scarlet mantle. Above his Helmet, upon his cuirass, and on his shoulder pieces and buskins he bears, as a crest, a winged black Horse's head. He grasps a Club with Flaming ends, somewhat similar to that in the symbol of the Ace of Wands, but not so heavy, and also the Sigil of his scale is shewn.

### THE FOUR QUEENS

Are seated upon Thrones, representing the Forces of Heh of the Name in each suit, the Mother, and bringer forth of material Force, a Force which develops, and realises the Force of the King. A Force steady and unshaken, but not rapid though enduring. It is therefore symbolised by a figure seated upon a Throne but also clothed in armour.

### THE FOUR KNIGHTS

These Knights (sometimes called Princes) are figures seated in chariots, and thus borne forward. The represent the Vau forces of the Name in each suit; the Mighty son of the King and the Queen, who realises the influence of both scales of Force. A prince, the son of a King and Queen, yet a Prince of Princes, and a King of Kings. An Emperor, whose effect is at once rapid (though not so swift as that of a king) and enduring (though not as steadfast as that of a queen). It is therefore symbolise by a figure borne in a chariot, and clothed with armour. Yet is his power illusionary, unless set in motion by his Father and Mother.

### THE FOUR PRINCESSES

These are also known as the Knaves. The Four Princesses or Figures of Amazons standing firmly by themselves, neither riding upon Horses, nor seated upon Thrones, nor borne on Chariots. They represent the forces of Heh final of the Name in each suit, completing the influences of the other scales. The mighty and potent daughter of a King and Queen: a Princess powerful and terrible. A Queen of Queens, an Empress, whose effect combines those of the King, Queen and Prince. At once violent and permanent, she is therefore symbolised by a figure

## THE RADIX POWERS OF THE EARTH
## ACE OF PENTACLES

A white radiant Angelic Hand, holding a branch of a Rose Tree, whereon is a large Pentacle, formed of five concentric circles. The innermost Circle is white, charged with a red Greek cross. From this white centre 12 white rays issue. These terminate at the circumference, making the whole something like an astrological figure of the Heavens.

It is surmounted by a small circle, above which is a large Maltese Cross, and with two white wings; four roses and two buds are shewn. The hand issueth from the clouds as in the other three cases. It representeth materiality in all senses, good and evil, and is therefore in a sense illusionary. It shows material gain, labour, power, wealth, etc.

## THE SIXTEEN COURT CARDS
## THE FOUR KINGS

The Four Kings of Figures mounted on Steeds. (This is very important due to the general confusion even in these papers between Kings and Knights; all Kings should be on horses and all Knights should be on thrones or chariots.) They represent the Yod forces of the Name in each suit, the Radix, Father, and commencement of Material Forces. A Force in which all the others are implied and of which they form the development and completion. A force swift and violent in action, but whose effect soon passes away, and therefore symbolised by a figure on a steed riding swiftly, and clothed in complete armour.

Therefore is the knowledge of the scale of the King so necessary for the commencement of all magical working.

And between it and that on the right, are twelve–six above and six below–about the left hand Branch. The whole is a great and Flaming Torch, symbolising force, strength, rush, vigour, energy, and it governs according to its nature various works and questions. It implies natural as opposed to Invoked Force.

## THE RADIX OF THE POWERS OF THE WATERS
## ACE OF CUPS

A radiant white Angelic Hand issuing from clouds and supporting on its palm a Cup, resembling that of the Solsistes. From it rises a fountain of clear and glistening Water; and spray falling on all sides into clear calm water below, in which grows Lotus and water lilies. The great letter Heh of the Supernal Mother is traced in the spray of the Fountain. It symbolises Fertility, Productiveness, Beauty, Pleasure, Happiness, etc.

## THE RADIX OF THE POWERS OF AIR
## ACE OF SWORDS

A white radiating Angelic Hand, issuing from clouds, and grasping the hilt of a Sword, which supports a white radiant celestial Crown from which depend, on the right, the olive branch of Peace, and on the left, the Palm branch of suffering. Six Vaus fall from its point. It symbolises invoked as contrasted with natural Forces; for it is the Invocation of the Sword. Raised upward, it invokes the Divine Crown of Spiritual Brightness. Reversed it is the invocation of demoniac force, and becomes a fearfully evil symbol. It represents therefore very great power for good or evil, but **invoked**. And it also represents whirling force, and strength through trouble. It is the affirmation of justice, upholding Divine authority; and it may become the Sword of Wrath, Punishment and Affliction.

# THE 78 TAROT CARDS
# THEIR DESCRIPTION AND MEANING

## THE ACES

The first in order and appearance are the four Aces, representing the force of the Spirit acting in, and binding together the four scales of each element and answering to the Dominion of the Letters of the Name in the Kether of each. They represent the Radical or Root-Force and are said to be placed on the North Pole of the Universe, where in they revolve, governing its revolution, and ruling as the connecting link between Yetzirah and Assiah.

## THE RADIX OF THE POWERS OF FIRE
## ACE OF WANDS

A white radiating Angelic Hand issuing from clouds and grasping a heavy Club which has three branches in the colours and with the Sigils of the Scales. The right and left hand branches end respectively in three Flames and the centre one in four Flames, thus yielding Ten the number of Sephiroth. Twenty two leaping Flames or Yods surround it, answering to the Paths. Three fall below the right branch for Aleph, Mem and Shin. Seven above the central branch for the double letters.

## Names and Attributions of the Remaining Minor Arcana

| Card | Lord of | Decan | Signs |
|---|---|---|---|
| 5 Wands | Strife | Saturn | Leo |
| 6 Wands | Victory | Jupiter | Leo |
| 7 Wands | Valour | Mars | Leo |
| 8 Pentacles | Prudence | Sun | Virgo |
| 9 Pentacles | Material Gain | Venus | Virgo |
| 10 Pentacles | Wealth | Mercury | Virgo |
| 2 Swords | Peace Restored | Moon | Libra |
| 3 Swords | Sorrow | Saturn | Libra |
| 4 Swords | Rest from Strife | Jupiter | Libra |
| 5 Cups | Loss in Pleasure | Mars | Scorpio |
| 6 Cups | Pleasure | Sun | Scorpio |
| 7 Cups | Illusionary Success | Venus | Scorpio |
| 8 Wands | Swiftness | Mercury | Sagittarius |
| 9 Wands | Great Strength | Moon | Sagittarius |
| 10 Wands | Oppression | Saturn | Sagittarius |
| 2 Pentacles | Harmonious Change | Jupiter | Capricorn |
| 3 Pentacles | Material Works | Mars | Capricorn |
| 4 Pentacles | Earthy Power | Sun | Capricorn |
| 5 Swords | Defeat | Venus | Aquarius |
| 6 Swords | Earned Success | Mercury | Aquarius |
| 7 Swords | Unstable Effort | Moon | Aquarius |
| 8 Cups | Abandoned Success | Saturn | Pisces |
| 9 Cups | Material Happiness | Jupiter | Pisces |
| 10 Cups | Perpetual Success | Mars | Pisces |
| 2 Wands | Dominion | Mars | Aries |
| 3 Wands | Established Strength | Sun | Aries |
| 4 Wands | Perfected Work | Venus | Aries |
| 5 Pentacles | Material Trouble | Mercury | Taurus |
| 6 Pentacles | Material Success | Moon | Taurus |
| 7 Pentacles | Success Unfulfilled | Saturn | Taurus |
| 8 Swords | Shortened Force | Jupiter | Gemini |
| 9 Swords | Despair and Cruelty | Mars | Gemini |
| 10 Swords | Ruin | Sun | Gemini |
| 2 Cups | Love | Venus | Cancer |
| 3 Cups | Abundance | Mercury | Cancer |
| 4 Cups | Blended Pleasure | Moon | Cancer |

## Names and Attributions of the Tarot Trumps

| Names | Titles | Hebrew | Signs |
|---|---|---|---|
| Fool | The Spirit of Ether. | Aleph | Air |
| Magician | The Magus of Power. | Beth | Mercury |
| High Priestess | Priestess of the Silver Star. | Gimel | Moon |
| Empress | Daughter of the Mighty Ones. | Daleth | Venus |
| Emperor | Son of the Morning, Chief among the Mighty. | Heh | Aries |
| Hierophant | Magus of the Eternal Gods. | Vau | Taurus |
| Lovers | Children of the Voice Divine, The Oracles of the Mighty Gods. | Zayin | Gemini |
| Chariot | Children of the Power of the Waters, Lord of the Triumph of Light. | Cheth | Cancer |
| Fortitude | Daughter of the Flaming Sword, Leader of the Lion. | Teth | Leo |
| Hermit | The Magus of the Voice of Light, The Prophet of the Gods. | Yod | Virgo |
| Wheel of Fortune | The Lord of the Forces of Life. | Caph | Jupiter |
| Justice | Daughter of the Lord of Truth, The Holder of the Balances. | Lamed | Libra |
| Hanged Man | The Spirit of the Mighty Waters. | Mem | Water |
| Death | The Child of the Great Transformers, Lord of the Gates of Death. | Nun | Scorpio |
| Temperance | Daughters of the Reconcilers, The Bringer Forth of Life. | Samekh | Sagittarius |
| Devil | Lord of the Gates of Matter, Child of the Forces of Time. | Ayin | Capricorn |
| Blasted Tower | Lord of the Hosts of the Mighty. | Peh | Mars |
| The Star | Daughter of the Firmament, Dweller between the Waters. | Tzaddi | Aquarius |
| The Moon | Ruler of Flux and Reflux, Child of the Sons of the Mighty. | Qoph | Pisces |
| The Sun | Lord of the Fire of the World. | Resh | Sun |
| Judgment | The Spirit of the Primal Fire. | Shin | Fire |
| Universe | The Great One of the Night of Time. | Tau | Saturn |

12. The Knave of Cups is The Princess of the Waters and the Lotus.
13. The King of Swords is The Lord of the Wind and the Breezes, The Lord of the Spirits of the Air.
14. The Queen of Swords is The Queen of the Thrones of the Air.
15. The Knight of Swords is The Prince of the Chariots of the Wind.
16. The Knave of Swords is The Princess of the Rushing Winds, The Lotus of the Palace of Air.
17. The King of Pentacles is The Lord of the Wide and Fertile land, King of the Spirits of the Earth.
18. The Queen of Pentacles is The Queen of the Thrones of Earth.
19. The Knight of Pentacles is The Prince of the Chariot of Earth.
20. The Knave of Pentacles is The Princess of the Echoing Hills, the Rose of the Palace of Earth.

## THE TITLES OF THE TAROT CARDS

1. Ace of Wands is called the Root of the Powers of Fire.
2. Ace of Swords is called the Root of the Powers of Air.
3. Ace of Pentacles is called the Root of the Powers of Earth.
4. Ace of Cups is called the Root of the Powers of Water.
5. The King of Wands is called the Lord of Flames and Lightning. The King of the Spirits of Fire.
6. The Queen of Wands is The Queen of the Thrones of Flames.
7. The Knight of Wands is The Prince of the Chariot of Fire.
8. The Knave of Wands is The Princess of the Shining Flame, and The Rose of the Palace of Fire.
9. The King of Cups is The Lord of the Waves and the Waters, and The King of the Hosts of the Sea.
10. The Queen of Cups is The Queen of the Thrones of Waters.
11. The Knight of Cups is The Prince of the Chariot of Waters.

## The Complete Golden Dawn System of Magic
By Israel Regardie[1]
### THE 78 TAROT CARDS
New Falcon Publications, First Edition 1984

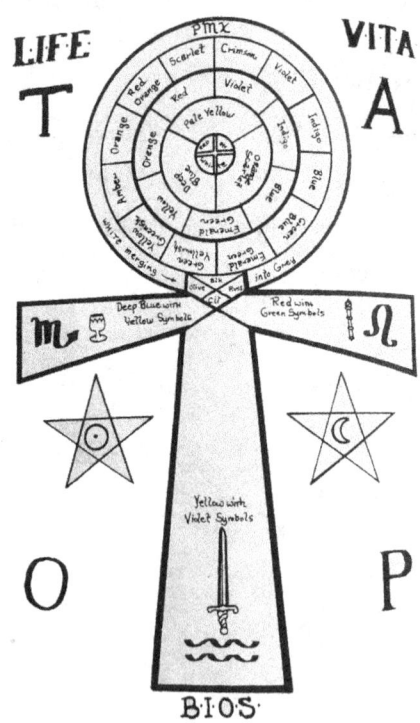

**Ankh of the Tarot**

nature in what this extraordinary man of genius has written and published. But I am also profoundly impressed by this fact. Unless one has first studied Magic from a more comprehensible and realiable source, most of what he has written, albeit based upon his own practical experience, will be in the main unintelligible. Any student who has gained a sympathetic understanding of the Golden Dawn teachng will be capable of discriminating between the futile reprehensible portions of Crowley's work, and of deciding which part of it is a worthwhile addition to an already magnificent system. And it is because Crowley concedes to his own credit in his, in many respects, admirable volume entitled Magick that he has done Magic inestimable service by reason of his development of it, that I have considered it imperative, together with a number of other reasons of urgency, to place the Golden Dawn system before the public. Crowley's claims are, in my estimation, wholly exaggerated. I am far from being convinced that the scheme of theory and practice presented in his literature–extraordinary though it is in many ways, considering that it is a development of the simple basic Golden Dawn material–is equal in any way to the system put into documentary form by S.L. MacGregor Mathers and his colleagues.

active Order. This is certainly true of the instruction, for example, on Geomancy. The rituals and teachings were badly mauled, rearranged out of all recognition to their former state, and then surrounded by Yoga instructions, short stories, articles on sex-Magic, poetry–much of it of dubious nature–and a host of miscellaneous odds and ends.

With Crowley's instructions in the art of Yoga, printed both within and without the *Equinox*, there can be no quarrel. They are amongst the clearest ever produced on the subject and amongst the finest examples of the excellent prose of which Crowley was capable. We, the occult-reading public, are immeasurably the richer for their appearance. Epigrams, short stories, card-games, and libels on former friends, however, can hardly be considered fit companions for occult teaching. It is my confirmed belief that it is practically impossible, without more precise guidance or tuition, to ascertain from the *Equinox* and Crowley's other literary productions exactly what is the actual nature of Magic as a definite practical scheme. His form of presentation, and the other contents of the *Equinox*, created nothing but confusion.

Though a revelation of the inner teaching of the Golden Dawn would have been a boon to mankind, yet manifestly Crowley's manner of presentation ruined the effort. If the breaking of a sacred oath is revealed in a dignified manner and with a noble spirit, as well as in a style fitting to its intrinsic nature. In such an event, the oath is neither betrayed nor profaned, for in being abrogated on behalf of mankind, the author becomes duly qualified to speak for those with whom alone is the power to bind or loose.

It is not my wish to retract what nearly three years ago I enthusiastically wrote in *The Tree of Life*. It was then my conviction as it is now that there was much of a highly important may have been the means fair or foul by which he obtained that teaching. And while he did not publish it in its entirety, it is possible to perceive from hints scattered here, there, and everywhere, that very little had been kept from him. Any student who has a bird's-eye view of the Order system will recognise traces of every aspect of it in the different volumes of Crowley's literary fecundity.

Had Crowley published the entire body of knowledge, only slightly editing the redundancy and verbose complexity of Mathers' literary style–had he issued that teaching so that it bore some semblance to its original state to indicate what it really was and how practiced within the Temple–his exposé might not have been too serious. It is possible that he might have been acknowledged as a benefactor of mankind, even if later on he did ruin his own personal reputation by broadcasting absurd lengths and leading a foolishly dissipated life. But it was his secret mode of publication which argued against the advisability of partially disclosing, the secret knowledge of the Order. He tampered unnecessarily with the Grade rituals, so that their beauty as well as practical worth was gone.[3] It became impossible to form any estimation of the efficacy or construction of those ceremonies from their manipulated shadows in the *Equinox*. Perhaps his aim was to eliminate important parts of the rites and practical work so that interested people, realising that more information was required, would communicate with him for further guidance, thus enabling him to consolidate his position as a leader, and formulate an

---

[3] It is statements like these that have led Crowley-deifiers to hate and ignore Regardie. Anyone who gives Crowley a fair read will find that much of what he wrote is pure crap. All too often his followers have elevated the garbage to a gospel while ignoring the good stuff. Such is the process of Biblification. In the world of organized religion, truth must be eliminated as a threat to self-aggrandizing dogma. [Ed.]

so great a laughing stock on that occasion as to make it difficult for anyone to take him seriously. The conjunction of two headstrong and egotistical personalities rendered it most probable that sooner or later Crowley and Mathers should quarrel. They did, and each went his separate way. Many and varied again are the fantastic accounts of the reasons for that separation. But no matter what their cause, some three years afterwards events led Crowley to denounce Mathers as one obsessed either by Abramelin demons or by the evil personalities of the then incarcerated Horos couple, and that he himself had been nominated by the Secret Chiefs of the Invisible Order to be the outer head of the visible organisation. In the various numbers of the Equinox, the official organ of Crowley's personal reformation of the Order system under the title of A∴A∴–which does not signify "Atlantean Adepts" as supposed by some stupid reviewer in the Occult Review–may be found Crowley's more or less garbled version of the Order teaching and ceremonial.

At this juncture, it is needful to contradict denials on the part of certain Order members that Crowley did not obtain full Order teaching. Some of these denials are entirely too vehement and "methinks the lady doth protest too much." First of all, I am fully convinced from a close and prolonged study of all Crowley's literary output that he did obtain his Adeptus Minor grade from Mathers after the London group refused to advance him. Unquestionably this is true. Nevertheless, even if this were not the case, he was the *intime*, so to say, of Fratres Volo Noscere and Yehi Aour, both advanced members of the grade of Adeptus Minor, who coached and trained him so that he benefited by their knowledge and wide experience. Whatever knowledge these Fratres had received from the Order documents, was given to Crowley. There is little, I imagine, that he did not receive of the Order teaching then extant, whatever assimilated the routine knowledge without the least difficulty. Those grades which were not formally separated by automatic delays, were taken at the rate of one a month, and the succeeding ones at the prescribed intervals of three, seven, and nine months. By the time he had taken his Portal grade, the revolt was in full swing, the wisdom and authority of the Chief being on every side doubted and challenged. It was around this period, too, that Crowley's morals and alleged pernicious conduct offended those who were conducting Temple work in London, and the ruling Adepti of Isis-Urania refused to advance him further. They refused to do this in spite of the deliberate warning contained in Mathers' manifesto previously mentioned: "What I discontenance and will check and punish whenever I find it in the Order is the attempt to criticise and interfere with the private life of members of the Order.... The private life of a person is a matter between himself or herself and his or her God." Whether Mathers was impressed by the promise of Crowley's personality, or whether he decided upon his next step to show contempt for the ruling Chiefs of Isis-Urania Temple, we do not know. But, soon after, Crowley was invited to Paris where he received the grade of Adeptus Minor from Mathers in Ahathoor Temple. This act served but to inflame the differences which were now openly separating Mathers from his erstwhile followers, and increased the bitter hatred which the Order members bore and still bear for Crowley.

To Crowley's credit, it must be conceded that when open revolt did flame forth, at least he sided with S.R.M.D., acting as his plenipotentiary in the proposed meetings with the rebels in London. The Adepti, however, unconditionally refused to recognise or have ought to do with Crowley. In his fantastic garb of a Highland chieftain with kilt, dirks and tartan, and his face concealed by a heavy mask, he did assuredly make himself

One can hardly help recalling the bitter admonition given by S.R.M.D. to the organisers of the schism. He said, in effect, and in later years Frater Sub Spe corroborated that statement, that he was the principal Chief of the Order by whom and through whom the Order had originally been organised to disseminate the magical tradition. Remember, he warned, what happened to the Theosophical Society after Blavatsky had departed, and there began the disintegration of the worldwide society she had founded and fed with her own life blood. Certainly Mathers' prophecy seems to have vindicated itself. Just as there are innumerable sects claiming to be the original Theosophical Society and professing allegiance to the principles taught by Blavatsky, so are there now several decaying Temples claiming unbroken descent from the original Isis-Urania. Each insists fervently that it alone is the genuine Order; all others are schismatic and unimportant. To-day as stated above, not one of these surviving Temples is in an even moderately healthy condition. Nor have they ever been since the early days of their foundation. An amusing sidelight on human nature is disclosed by the fact that in one of the Obligations retained by the schismatic groups, there is still the original clause, "Do you further undertake not to be a stirrer of strife, of schism, or of opposition to the Chiefs."

It was towards the close of 1898, just prior to the revolt, that Aleister Crowley was introduced to the Order by Frater Volo Noscere, receiving his Neophyte initiation at Mark Mason's Hall. It was clear, soon after he joined, that here was a highly gifted young man, and that in many ways, though unrestrained and undisciplined, his was a powerfully magical personality. From Captain J.F.C. Fuller's rather verbose and flamboyant account in the Equinox we gather that Crowley was advanced through the grades of the Order quickly, and name. In London also, a separate Temple was being conducted by Frater Sacramentum Regis calling itself the Reconstructed Rosicrucian Order, a group characterised by its exclusive devotion to Christian Mysticism, its rituals being elaborated into verbose and interminable parades of turgidity.

Formally united by a single fraternal bond, we now see several Temples being conducted by different groupings of individuals who, while pretending to fraternal communion, had but little sympathy with and affection for the sister Temples of the schism. The slander that was invented and swiftly circulated, as only malice can be circulated, is unrepeatable. Few individuals of real worth were exempt from this network of scandal which enmeshed the whole organisation. This man was an adulterer, that a dipsomaniac–and even after the lapse of more than thirty years this slander is still current. So thoroughly had the central unity of the Order broken up that each of these Stella Matutina Temples appointed its own Imperator, Cancellarius and Praemonstrator, considering itself by these gestures an autonomous occult body. Thus began the downfall of organised magical instruction through the semi-esoteric channels of the Hermetic Order of the Golden Dawn. Whatever else should be insisted upon in Magic, unity is the prime essential. A united body of manifestation at all costs should have been maintained. And the old adage "United we stand, divided we fall" is no idle phrase, especially since the elimination of the "heresy of separateness" is one of the cardinal injunctions of the Great Work. The separate temples decided to fall independently of how or why or where the other groups fell. Each was smug, complacent and fully confident that it alone continued the magical tradition. The result is that to-day those original Temples are either dead or moribund. While they may have given rise to yet other groups, there is not one of the latter which is not in diseased condition.

chose to resign. At the meetings held to appoint his succcessor, differences of the most trivial character continued to arise. Indeed, the spirit of fraternity and wisdom had departed, leaving its averse antithesis, the venom of destruction, to dwell in their midst. Another split developed. Apparently one wing of the schism, thoroughly alarmed in all its bourgeois incompetence and fear by the recent disturbances to the peace of the Order, attributed that cycle of catastrophe to the occult content of the Order teaching, and because of this were now desirous of casting aside as valueless, from the spiritual point of view, the whole of the magical tradition. Their intention was to retain a sort of indeterminate Mysticism of the type which has so often brought disrepute upon the subject, coming to regard their Temple as an adjunct, a clandestine back-door to the Church in some one of its many forms–with especial attractions, I believe, to the Anglo-Catholic groups. One other and more important group within the schism, led by Fratres Finem Respice and Sub Spe carried on full Temple work, more or less adhering to the original plan of the Golden Dawn routine as laid down in the documents drawn up by MacGregor Mathers.

Thus we find in place of a consolidated fraternity at last three separate groupings of individuals engaged in the practice of the Golden Dawn ceremonial system in open Temple, perpetuating as best they might the traditions of the Magic of Light. There was, first, the diminuative group under the leadership of S.R.M.D., still retaining the original Order name. To him were still loyal the Temple or Temples that a few years prior to the final crash had been instituted in the United States of America. Both F.R. and S.S. were in charge of a Stella Matutina Temple, and it is my belief that after a while even they parted company or conducted separate groups, the one in London calling itself the Amoun Temple, and the latter in Edinburgh, Amen-Ra by large extent the history of the Order is so confused and muddled at this juncture, and the rumours which have come down to us so chaotic and contradictory, that it has proved wholly impossible to extricate the truth from the foul débris of slander, abuse and recrimination. A clear picture of what occurred seems impossible to recover. It would appear, to state the matter simply, that Mathers expelled the rebels who then formed a schism. On the other hand, it is also held that he was himself expelled by the revolting wing from his own Order and left with about half a dozen adherents, with whose assistance, moral and financial, he continued his Temple.

As the first magical gesture of independence, the rebels changed the name of the Order to The Stella Matutina. Ruled for a year by a committee of twelve, developments forced them to realise that this was far from a satisfactory arrangement. Inasmuch, however, as it had taken several years first to brew and then to develop into an open gesture of defiance, the spirit which had conceived the rebellion was not thus at a single stroke to be banished. Having elevated the standard of revolt by expelling their former chief, for many a dismal month was the Stella Matutina haunted by that ghost. After almost inconceivable pettiness and dispute, the rebels were at the end persuaded by circumstance to abandon every feature of their reform to return to the original scheme of appointing Three Chiefs to govern and lead them. Even this, later, was abandones if not officially then in practice, for a virtual autocracy similar to that enjoyed by Mathers was once again instituted, though on a much smaller scale. The revolt had been in vain. Those finally selected and appointed as the Chiefs were Fratres Sub Spe, Finem Respice, and Sacramentun Regis. These three Fratres conducted the Order of the Stella Matutina in harmony for about a year. Then, for various reasons, Sacramentum Regis statement that S.A. had never been at any time in touch with Fräulein Sprengel of Nüremberg but had "either himself forged or procured to be forged the professed correspondence between him and her." As was only to be expected this letter came as an overwhelming surprise to S.S.D.D.,who was thoroughly stunned by this accusation of dishonesty and forgery levelled against S.A. After contemplating the whole situation in an almost frantic state of mind for several days in the country, she finally communicated with S.A. asking him to corroborate or deny the accusations. her next act was to form a Committee of Seven within the Second Order to investigate the allegations made. This Committee asked S.R.M.D. to produce for his own sake and for the sake of the Order proof of the accuracy of his statements. Because, they argued, since it was upon the authority of this alleged correspondence that the Order was founded, the historical position of the Order as descended from mediaeval Rosicrucian sources collapsed should it be proven that the correspondence had been forged. This viewpoint was not altogether accurate, for while S.R.M.D. had stated that S.A. had never been in touch with S.D.A., he never denied that he himself had not been in constant communication with her. Then followed a lengthy correspondence which afterwards was collected and printed in the form of a long dossier. In fine, Mathers refused unconditionally to acknowledge the authority or even the existence of the Committee nor would he produce proof of any kind to substantiate his claim that S.A. had forged Second Order communications. It goes without saying of course that S.A. fervently denied the truth of those allegations of forgery, but all the same he refused to do anything about it.

No good purpose could possibly be served by enlarging upon the unhappy events which immediately followed. To a her status. Anyway, it was a sad piece of deception, and an unhappy acknowledgment on the part of Mathers indicating his complete lack of judgment and insight into character. Mrs. Horos and her husband were very soon discovered to be sex-perverts of the worst description. Nor was this all, for it is alleged that they were also responsible for the theft from Mathers of a complete set of Order documents. It seems incredible that Mathers could have been so gullible, for that is the word which adequately describes his stupidity, as to accept without further verification the occult claims of this woman, giving her access to the rituals and teaching of the Golden Dawn. Subsequently the immoral activities of these two people having attracted the attention of the police, they were arrested. In December 1901 at their trial, the Order of the Golden Dawn was given unpleasant and unjustified publicity by being associated with the chequered career of these two persons. In the witness box the male prisoner made the remark concerning the Golden Dawn Neophyte obligation that it "was prepared by the Chief of the Order who are in India"–which of course was a farrago of nonsense, but unfortunately just the type of nonsense which survives for many years. He was sentenced to fifteen years penal servitude, and his wife to seven.

Around this period also, one Florence Farr, whose esoteric motto was Soror S.S.D.D., having for some years been left in charge of Isis-Urania Temple while Mathers continued to research work in Paris, decided for various personal reasons to enter her resignation from that important post. Under date of of February 16th 1900, Mathers, writing from Paris, refused to accept her resignation, believing that she intended to "form a combination to make a schism therein with the idea of working secretly or avowedly under Sapere Aude." In this same letter, he was responsible for the astonishing

In claiming his right to unquestioned leadership, and when refusing to appoint two others of the body of Adepti to fill the vacant posts of co-Chiefs, Mathers also promised some of the more advanced members of the Second Order additional grades in the path of Adeptship and even ore esoteric teaching. These, apparently, were not forthcoming–though it must be confessed that regardless of the personal shortcomings of Mathers as a leader or as a writer, it is patent that there was a vast knowledge and a deep and wide erudition concealed with him. Naturally the Adepti gave utterance to their complete disapproval of this delay in the fulfilment of their Chief's promises, gradually coming to insist that he had neither the knowledge nor the grades to impart. Further unpleasant bickering drew forth from Mathers the retort that he was certainly not going to waste either their grades or knowledge on such hopeless duffers as they were. And in any event, he was Chief and leader; their further progress, if there was to be any, must be left entirely in his hands. In short, a virulent quarrel was in process of development, and though for quite a long time it fermented beneath the surface, it finally culminated in a group of the Adepti forming a strong combination to expel their chief S.R.M.D. just prior to the actual appearance of the schism, and whilst yet the rebellion was gaining impetus, certain events happened which call here not for elucidation, since that is impossible, but simply for registration.

About this time, a certain Mrs. Rose Horos approached Mathers who came to acknowledge her as an initiate of a high grade. Exactly why, it is again impossible to say definitely. It was stated in defence of Mathers that Mrs. Horos was able to repeat to him a certain conversation he had had years previously when he visited Madame Blavatsky at Denmark Hill, and the repetition of this scrap of conversation convinced him of occurrence, he issued to the Theorici of the grade of Adeptus Minor a powerfully worded manifesto, naming himself in no uncertain terms as a chosen vessel and demanding from all those who received the manifesto a signed oath of personal loyalty and allegiance. Those who refused to send a written statement of voluntary submission to him were either expelled from the Order or degraded to a lower rank.

Meanwhile, a considerable amount of discontent had been slowly brewing amongst the Order members. Dissatisfaction with the autocratic leadership of S.R.M.D. was growing very steadily and persistently. No definite or clear-cut reasons appear to be given for this, for evidently this restlessness had been gradually fructifying whilst the hypertrophy of Mather's ego was becoming more and more pronounced. Some say that S.R.M.D. was guilty of innumerable magical tricks of a particularly irresonsible nature which eventually brought disrepute both upon himself and the Order of which he was head. Others, more romantically minded, claimed that his English translation of *The Sacred Magic of Abramelin the Mage* was a powerful magical act which attracted to his sphere forces of evil so terrible in nature that he was wholly unable to withstand them. Frater F.R. propounds the more rational view that it was simply spiritual pride and love of power which so gained the ascendancy that he demanded of the members of his organisation a personal fealty and obedience to his own personality instead of to the work itself. How very familiar all this sounds? In one form or another, it is the story of the same unhappy fate which dogs and finally ruins every religious and spiritual community. By changing these names, Theosophists may recognise a very homely story.[2]

---

[2] As may knowledgeable, modern-day students of the Golden Dawn.

manuscripts in a portfolio bearing his signature in a cab, and the driver upon finding them turned them over to the authorities. Since Westcott was by profession an East London coroner, the medical authorities strongly objected that one in an official capacity should, no matter how remotely, he connected with anything that savoured occult. It was suggested to him therefore that the must withdraw from the Order or else resign his post as coroner, since the two were considered in those days incompatibles. He chose to resign from the Order. Yet again it is suggested that it was simply a personal quarrel that led to the parting of the ways with Mathers, which does deem the more probable explanation. Whatever the cause, some six years after the death of Dr. Woodman, Westcott withdrew from the Order, which was thus left to the sole authority of Mathers.

The pamphlet on Rosicrucian history then proceeds in narrative that following Westcott's resignation from "this association in 1897, the English Temple soon after fell into abeyance." This reads like an instance of wish-fulfillment. Though fairly near the essential truth of the matter, it is not quite in accordance with fact. Following the resignation of Westcott, Mathers reigned within his Order as supreme autocrat. Judging from the evidence at our disposal he was not a particularly benevolent one, for many were the misunderstandings that ruffled the mystic placidity of his Temples, and several of the individuals who dared so much to differ or argue with him were promptly expelled, and flung into the outer darkness. Presumably spiritual pride was the flaw in the armour, and he seemed to harbour quite a few delusions. One of the latter was his conveyance to the body of Adepti as a piece of objective everyday experience, that whilst in the Bois de Boulogne one day he was approached by three Adepts who confirmed him in the sole rulership of the Order. On the strength of his supposed in London, Bradford, Weston-super-Mare, and Edinburgh. The ceremonies we have were elaborated from cipher manuscripts, and all went well for a time."

As to what ensued after that inauguration of Temple work here we have little record, though an unorthodox account written by Aleister Crowely continues this historical theme in substantially the same words as were orally communicated to me by the late Imperator of one of the now-existent Temples. "After some time S.D.A. died; further requests for help were met with a prompt refusal from the colleagues of S.D.A. It was written by one of them that S.D.A.'s schemes had always been regarded with disapproval but since the absolute rule of the Adepts is never to interfere with the judgment of any other person whomsoever–how much more, then, one of themselves, and that one most highly revered!–they had refrained from active opposition. The Adept who wrote this added that the Order had already quite enough knowledge to enable it or its members to formulate a magical link with the adepts. Shortly after this, one called S.R.M.D. announced that he had formulated such a link, and that himself with two others was to govern the Order... We content ourselves, then, with observing that the death of one of his two colleagues, and the weakness of the other, secured to S.R.M.D., the sole authority..."

In elaboration of this statemen, it may be said that in 1891 Dr. Woodman died after but a few days illness, leaving the management of the Order to Westcott and Mathers. Evidently these two scholars carried on quite well together for about six years, for the indications are that the Order flourished and grew exapansive. Exactly why Westcott withdrew from the Order–for this is the next major occurrence–appears difficult to discover. Concerning this also several versions are extant. One account has it that accidently he left some of the Order and a comprehensive scheme of spiritual training. Its foundation was designed to include both men and women on a basis of perfect equality in contradistinction to the policy of the Societas Rosicruciana in Anglia which was comprised wholly of Freemasons. Thus, in 1887, the Hermetic Order of the Golden Dawn was established. Its first English Temple, Isis-Urania, was opened in the following year.

There is somewhat different version as to its origin, having behind it the authority of Frater F.R. the late Dr. Felkin, who was the Chief of the Stella Matutina as well as a member of the Societas Rosicruciana. According to his account, and the following words are substantially his own, prior to 1880 members of the Rosicrucian Order on the Continent selected with great care their own candidates whom they thought suitable for personal instruction. For these pupils they were each individually responsible, the pupils thus selected being trained by them in the theoretical traditional knowledge now used in the Outer Order. After some three or more years of intensive private study they were presented to the Chiefs of the Order, and if approved and passed by examination, they then received their initiation into the Order of the Roseae Rubeae et Aureae Crucis.

The political state of Europe in those days was such that the strictest secrecy as to the activities of these people was very necessary. England, however, where many Masonic bodies and semi-private organisations were flourishing without interference, was recognised as having far greater freedom and liberty than the countries in which the continental Adepts were domiciled. Some, but by no means all, suggested therefore that in England open Temple work might be inaugurated. And Dr. Felkin here adds, though without the least word of explanation as to what machinery was set in motion towards the attainment of that end, "and so it was…It came about then that Temples arose enlightenment and extended powers of the human senses, especially in the directions of clairvoyance and clairaudience."

The first Chief of this Society, its Supreme Magus so-called, was one Robert Wentworth Little, who is said to have rescued some old rituals from a certain Masonic storeroom, and it was from certain of those papers that the Society's rituals were elaborated. He died in 1878, and in his stead was appointed Dr. William R. Woodman. Both Dr. Westcott and MacGregor Mathers were prominent and active members of this body. In fact, the former became Supreme Magus upon Woodman's death, the office of junior Magus being conferred upon Mathers. One legend has it that one day Westcott discovered in his library a series of cipher manuscripts, and in order to decipher them he enlisted the aid of MacGregor Mathers. It is said that this library was that of the Societas Rosicruciana in Anglia, and it is likewise asserted that those cipher manuscripts were among the rituals and documents originally rescued by Robert Little from Freemason's Hall. Yet other accounts have it that Westcott found the manuscripts on a bookstall in Farringdon Street. Further apocryphal legends claim that they were found in the library of books and manuscripts inherited from the mystic and clairvoyant, Frederick Hockley who died in 1885. Whatever the real origin of these mysterious cipher manuscripts, when eventually deciphered with the aid of MacGregor Mathers, they were alleged to have contained the address of Fräulein Anna Sprengel who purported to be a Rosicrucian Adept, in Nüremburg. Here was a discovery which, naturally, not for one moment was neglected. Its direct result was a lengthy correspondence with Fräulein Sprengel, culminating in the transmission of authority to Woodman, Westcott and Mathers, to formulate in England a semi-public occult organisation which was to employ an elaborate magical ceremonial, Qabalistic teaching,

Mathers, the translator of *The Greater Key of King Solomon*, the *Book of the Sacred Magic of Abramelin the Mage*, and *The Qabalah Unveiled*, which latter consisted of certain portions of the Zohar prefixed by an introduction of high erudition. He also employed the *inabitur* Astris chosen by a Fräulein Anna Sprengel of Nüremberg, Germany. Such were the actors on this occult stage, this the *dramatis personae* in the background of the commencement of the Order. More than any other figures who may later have prominently figured in its government and work, these are the four outstanding figures publicly involved in the English foundation of what came to be known as The Hermetic Order of the Golden Dawn.

How the actual beginning came to pass is not really known. Or rather, because of so many conflicting stories and legends the truth is impossible to discover. At any rate, so far as England is concerned, without a doubt we must seek for its origins in the Societas Rosicruciana in Anglia. This was an organization formulated in 1865 by eminent Freemasons, some of them claiming Rosicrucian initiation from continental authorities. Amongst those who claimed such initiation was one Kenneth Mackenzie, a Masonic scholar and encyclopaedist, who had received his at the hands of a Count Apponyi in Austria. The objects of his Society, which confined its membership to Freemasons in good standing, was to "afford mutual aid and encouragement in working out the great problems of Life, and in discovering the secrets of nature; to facilitate the study of the systems of philosophy founded upon the Kaballah and the doctrines of Hermes Trismegistus." Dr. Westcott also remarks that to-day's Fratres "are concerned in the study and administration of medicines, and in their manufacture upon old lines; they also teach and practise the curative effects of coloured light, and cultivate mental processes which are believed to induce spiritual

The membership of the Golden Dawn was recruited from every circle, and it was represented by dignified professions as well as by all the arts and sciences, to make but little mention of the philosophers; and normal men and women, humble and unknown, from every walk of life have drawn inspiration from its font of wisdom, and undoubtedly many would be happy to recognise and admit the enormous debt they owe to it.

As an organisation, it preferred always to shroud itself in an impenetrable cloak of mystery. Its teaching and methods of instruction were stringently guarded by various penalties attached to the most awe-inspiring obligations in order to ensure that secrecy. So well have these obligations with but one or two exceptions been kept that the general public knows next to nothing about the Order, its teaching, or the extent and nature of its membership. Though this book will touch upon the teaching of the Golden Dawn, concerning its membership as a whole the writer will have nothing to say, except perhaps to repeat what may already be more or less well-know. For instance, it is common knowledge that W.B. Yeats, Arthur Machen and, if rumour may be trusted, the late Arnold Bennett were at one time among its members, together with a good many other writers and artists.

With regard to the names given in Dr. Westcott's statement it is necessary that we bestow to them some little attention in order to unravel, so far as may be possible, the almost inextricable confusion which has characterised every previous effort to detail the history of the Order. M.E.V. was the motto chosen by Dr. William Robert Woodman, an eminent Freemason of the last century. *Sapere Aude* and *Non Omnis Moriar* were the two mottos used by Dr. Westcott, an antiquarian, scholar, and coroner by profession. S.R.M.D. or S. Rhiogail Ma Dhream was the motto of S.L. MacGregor

Hermetic Science and the higher Alchemy from a long series of practiced investigators whose origin in traced to the Fratres Roseae Crucis of Germany, which association was founded by one Christian Rosenkreutz about the year 1398 A.D....

"The Rosicrucian revival of Mysticism was but a new development of the vastly older wisdom of the Qabalistic Rabbis and of that very ancient secret knowledge, the Magic of the Egyptians, in which the Hebrew Pentateuch tells you that Moses, the founder of the Jewish system was 'learned', that is, in which he had been initiated." In a slender but highly informative booklet entitled *Data of the History of the Rosicrucians* published in 1916 by the late Dr. William Wynn Westcott, we find the following brief statement: "In 1887 by permission of S.D.A. [Anna Sprengel] a continental Rosicrucian Adept, the Isis-Urania Temple of Hermetic Students of the G.D. was formed to give instruction in the mediaeval Occult sciences. Fratres M.E.V. [William Robert Woodman] with S.A. [Dr. Wynn Westcott] and S.R.M.D. [S.L. MacGregor Mathers] became the chiefs, and the latter wrote the rituals in modern English from old Rosicrucian mss. (the property of S.A.) supplemented by his own literary researches."

In these two statements is narrated the beginning of the Hermetic Order of the Golden Dawn–an organization which has exerted a greater influence on the development of Occultism since its revival in the last quarter of the 19th century than most people can realise. There can be little or no doubt that the Golden Dawn is, or rather was until very recently, the sole depository of magical knowledge, the only Occult Order of any real worth that the West in our time has known, and a great many other occult organisations owe what little magical knowledge is theirs to leakages issuing from that Order and from its renegade members.

# INTRODUCTION
# HISTORY OF THE GOLDEN DAWN
*The Complete Golden Dawn System of Magic*
THE EARLY YEARS
By Israel Regardie[1]
New Falcon Publications, First Edition 1984

"The Order of the Golden Dawn," narrates the history lecture of that Order, "is a Hermetic Society whose members are taught the principles of Occult Science and the Magic of Hermes. During the early part of the second half of last century, several eminent Adepti and Chiefs of the Order in France and England died, and their death caused a temporary dormant condition of Temple work.

"Prominent among the Adepti of our Order and of public renown, were Eliphas Lévi the greatest of modern French magi; Ragon, the author of several books of occult lore; Kenneth M. Mackenzie, author of the famous and learned Masonic Encyclopaedia and Frederick Hockley possessed of the power of vision in the crystal, and whose manuscripts are highly esteemed. These and other contemporary Adepti of this Order received their knowledge and power from predessors of equal and even of greater eminence. They received indeed and have handed down to us their doctrine and system of Theosophy and

---

[1] Originally published in *My Rosicrucian Adventure* (1936) which was revised and republished as *What You Should Know About the Golden Dawn* (Falcon Press, 1983).

pertains to the alchemical work are reviewed and related to the task at hand.

Where the earlier generations of alchemists would have been surprised and undoubtedly pleased, is in the sophisticated utilization of all modern pedagogic methods. Visual aids are employed in addition to oral instruction, plus frequent laboratory demonstrations. Some students who have previously acquainted themselves with the classical literature, have frequently remarked that a mere five minutes in the laboratory with a modern alchemist clarifies brilliantly what years of faltering, difficult reading and study never came to reveal.

Admittedly what is written here is superficial to a degree, but it may demonstrate to some degree the significance of the title of this article—that there *is* alchemy in modern times. It has never perished.

The "Lesser Work" is taught there prior, of course, to the "Magnum Opus," the "Great Work." And this naturally follows along classical lines. Herbs of all types are studied—from the picking and drying process, to that of extracting tinctures and similar final products. This is evidence of mere dilettantism. The work with metals and minerals is a necessary consequence of such investigations, but first things must come first. The metal and mineral operations have to follow in due course of time when the knowledge of the lesser work or circulation has been wholly mastered.

It might be well to emphasize here that respect for current laws is sternly inculcated. Students are not taught to diagnose or to prescribe for other people in violation of medical practice acts of the State. But they are taught to study themselves—since one's most outstanding task is to know oneself—and then to prepare a variety of herbal extracts and tinctures for themselves alone. The motive for such experimental work is to alter and raise their waves and frequencies so that they may be conscious participators in the great work of facilitating the onward progress of nature. But this work, like charity, must begin at home, with the student himself.

In addition to the practical work in the laboratory where alchemical processes are demonstrated and confirmed, there is also classroom work of lectures and study. Certain subjects are an absolute pre-requisite to laboratory experiment in order to arrive at a theoretical understanding of the laws of nature and so to appreciate what proceeds, as it were, in the test-tube. These subjects are astrology, known here as astro-cyclic pulsations; the Qabalah (which is an archaic mystical system with a mathematical structure long in use by the earlier alchemists); and, of course, much more about herbalism. Where and when necessary a few of the basic principles of metallurgy as it of alchemy and alchemists into the open. More than that, what has only recently occurred may never perhaps have been repeated. An actual school is in operation where the time-honored processes of alchemy are taught to carefully screened students. These are from all walks of life, from all levels of society, and with educations that vary from those with little to those with multiple university degrees. Here is definitely disproved the popular notion that alchemy was the unscientific mother of some of our modern sciences. The processes taught there as chemistry and physics are taught in our better colleges—by experiment, demonstration and experience. In beautifully equipped laboratories—where pyrex glassware and stainless steel accoutrements would have dazzled the classical scholars of former ages—there is a recrudescence of alchemical technique and process such as the world has never previously seen.

Nor is this merely a local phenomenon. Alchemy is once more rearing its head not only in this vast country of ours, but in Great Britain and in the heart of Europe as well, and in the Antipodes. There is communication now-a-days between its advocates as there always has been, since many of the famous published texts were simply the means whereby one adept in the art could convey to others somethings of his own knowledge and experience.

One school, perhaps the most prominent ever, The Paracelsus Research Society, has embarked on a most ambitious program which, punctuated by a Quarterly Bulletin and frequent publications, shows every sign of achieving fulfillment. Some of its books have achieved poly-lingual publication. Two of the most recent in the German tongue are *Prakitische alchemie im Zwanzigsten Jahrhundert* and *Men and the Cycles of the Universe*, both by Frater Albertus. Not a great deal of time elapses before first editions of all the books are exhausted.

be exercised in expressing what they believed or knew to be true. Often, then they used a scintillating variety of symbols and an even more exotic cosmological theory which, though considered defective and archaic from the point of view of twentieth century scientific philosophy, nonetheless enabled them to work out a satisfactory scheme of mythology. The latter, incidentally, is a word covering all our philosophy and psychology as well as our scientific theory. Anyway, in that mythology the above-mentioned ideas could be expressed and recognized as valid by others similarly engaged.

Having mentioned the term "mythology," it is worth while to remember the concluding remarks of E. J. Holmyard in his "Introductory" to his historical work on alchemy. "It may be recollected that the theory of the unity of the world permeated by a universal spirit had a corollary in the assumption that every object in the universe possessed some sort of life. Metals grew, as did minerals, and were even attributed sex. A fertilized seed of gold could develop into a nugget, the smoky exhalation was masculine and the vaporous one feminine, and mercury was a womb in which embryonic metals could be gestated. These and similar animistic beliefs mingle with the more rational outlook of Aristotle, and are more closely related to late forms of "Platonism."

I wonder whether these ideas are so outrageous as they once seemed to so many! The twentieth century, poised on the brink of the technology of multiple plastics, the exploration of space and fantastic feats of engineering, is about ready to accept a mythology or a philosophy which at first sight seems far more fantastic than that espoused by the old alchemists.

Today, the threat of persecution at the hands of vested religious or scientific interests has passed, thus permitting, perhaps for the first time in centuries of social history, the reemergence softly and quietly at the time. Its vibrations however, may permeate every nook and cranny of the scientific community before too long.

Because I sincerely think this may be well the case, I have taken the liberty of contributing this article on Alchemy in modern times. We are obliged to take the subject seriously and we have to recognize that thought it may now be accepted by only a few hundred people at the very most, yet they may turn out to be the spiritual and intellectual revolutionaries who are going to turn the whole scientific world topsy-turvy before it is capable of expanding its present limited point of view.

The alchemists of olden time were spiritually enlightened—not merely blind and stupid workers or seekers in the chemistry laboratory. This fact must never be forgotten. They sought to perfect *all* phases of man—his body, his mind, and his spirit. No one of these aspects of the total organism should be neglected. It was their belief that man is indefinitely perfectable. They were highly religious, and not disposed to deceive and swindle the treasury of the country in which they lived.

"Art perfects what nature began." Man, and all the gross and subtle constituents of nature, are capable of being brought to a state of infinite perfection. But nature unaided fails to achieve this perfection. Evolution may ultimately succeed, though the time factor seems so preposterously slow when one watches through recorded history, the cumbersome, the appallingly slow, progress of mankind. So the alchemists sought to intervene by their art—to speed up the process of growth and evolution, and so to aid God's work.

Since organized religion for the greater part of the last couple of thousand years would have denounced this heretical point of view and condemned its advocates to the torture rack and to the fiery stake, great care and caution at all times had to major interests without a break, but at the same time not only to imbue him with more vitality and energy but to aim for the highest spiritual goals.

About a decade ago, an alchemical manifesto was issued, completely out of the blue, unheralded and unannounced—and largely unnoticed. It announced that the alchemist's goals and techniques were once made available for study, research and consultation. It stated that "whereas the term Alchemy is associated by most people solely with the Philosophers Stone, and the making of Gold, it becomes necessary to correct this false notion. Alchemy, as such, covers an enormous territory and consists of the raising of the vibrations. This varied and many sided manifestation is the outcome of profound study and contemplation...In this new cycle of Alchemistical awakening it likewise becomes essential to commence cautiously our work, while making contact with those of like mind and aspirations, that may have been laying dormant for many years..."

Every now and again, I cannot help but be reminded of the Communist Manifesto issued by Karl Marx over a century ago. At the time of its issuance, very few people took serious notice of it—at best it was lightly dismissed as the ravings of madman. It may still be for all that. Nevertheless, whether you like it or not, the world has seen momentous changes in the entire social and economic structure as a definite result of that piece of paper. It has never been the same since—nor will it ever. In much that same way, I have the profound suspicion that before too much time has passed, this obscure Alchemistical Manifesto, noticed only by a few people within this country or the world at large, may begin to exert a greater influence on human minds and spirits than can possibly be conceived at this moment. It was a statement that was spoken

Before it is concluded that the alchemists were quacks and deceivers, we might remember the remark made by E.J. Holmyard, one of the more erudite and thoroughgoing historians of alchemy. "It must be remembered," he wrote, "that to the alchemists was due much of the practical chemical knowledge upon which scientific chemistry was based..." This disposes of the notion that they were ignorant. Furthermore, Holmyard, quoting from Boerhaave, a Dutch chemist of the early 18th century, the author of "New Method of Chemistry," adds:

"Wherever I understand the alchemists, I find them to describe the truth in the most simple and naked terms, without deceiving us, or being deceived themselves. When therefore I come to places, where I do not comprehend the meaning, why should I charge them with falsehood, who have shown themselves so much better skill'd in the art than myself?...Credulity is hurtful, so is incredulity; the business therefore of a wise man is to try all things, hold fast to what is approv'd, never limit the power of God, nor assign bounds to nature."

Whenever I hear references to alchemy made by people who obviously know nothing either of the literary or technical processes involved, I devoutly bless Boehaave in his quiet wisdom, wishing that our contemporary critics and scoffers could be half as sagacious as he.

Popular fancy has it that the old alchemists were primarily interested in one subject, and that only—the transmutation of base metals into gold. While there is little doubt that this may well have been true—enough texts are extant to substantiate this in part—nonetheless it must be stated categorically that this was merely one of its several goals. A closer examination of some of its important authorities indicates that they were also interested in healing mankind of some of its grosser ills, to substantially prolong human life so that one might pursue his

## ALCHEMY IN THE WORLD TODAY
By Israel Regardie

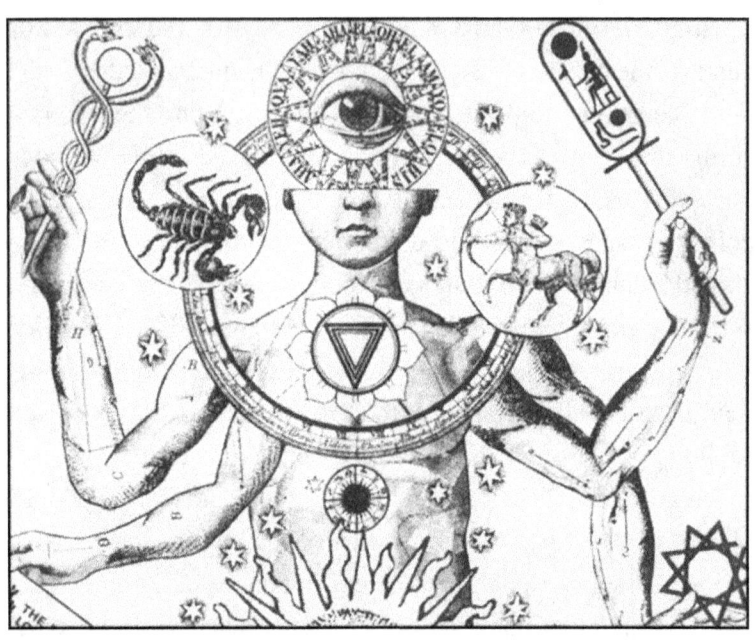

It may come as a distinct surprise to some to learn that the above heading is really a possibility. Alchemy was supposed to be an outgrown and discarded medieval art, the parent of present day chemistry which, as all know, is transforming our lives in such a wide variety of ways. Like many other current beliefs, this belief is far from the case. Alchemy may have spawned modern chemistry, but the fact remains it has never ceased to be a distinct science in its own right. It has always existed, and still does.

been engendered. Compelled, man will have found the God who abides in the heart of nature. That is a perfection which surely can overcome all problems and difficulties life may present—for the whole person and not simply their parts would be called into active operation. This would truly be evolution, and spiritual development and unfoldment in the finest and highest sense of term. Metaphysics, if wisely employed, can well become the technique of the future man.

The prayer gesture, therefore, aims to link many by aspiration or by suggestion to the whole vital world of former time when the world was young. That is why prayers and psalms of centuries ago seem to possess so great an efficacy. All harp on the great fundamental truths concerning the power of God in that He created the world, governs it now, and controls all its phenomena. And He can bless His creatures with fruition when they acknowledge Him, as is testified to by so many of the biblical narratives. Thus these prayers tend suggestively to connect the individual today, with events and individuals and divine manifestations of time gone by. If God did so much for Abraham and Solomon and Jesus in those days by virtue of their knowledge of Him, then likewise He can do as much today for me if I follow similar rules as did these men of old. A complex process of auto-suggestion is thus set into operation when the requisite degree of exaltation or concentration—the royal effective roads into the Unconscious—have been achieved. And the contemplation of these blessings and wonders evoke similar conditions from within where God abides.

emotions upon all the objects of his or her world, and not understanding themselves within, the things their environment presented were similarly primitive and savage and terrifying. It was necessary, as evolution and development proceeded, to break up this *participation mystique*, so that in the rejection of unconscious image-projection the mind would divorce itself from nature and be enormously improved and enriched.

But we have gone too far. The swing of the pendulum has carried us to the opposite extreme. Now we are afraid to see any kind of intelligence in nature outside of our own. We have developed mind to the extent that we have lost sight of the seedling world of unconscious forces within. We have strayed from our roots, and we are lost and stranded with no real sense of direction or guidance. The mind that we evolved has turned out to be, by itself, an empty bubble. Chained to the rock of our isolation like Prometheus, the vultures gnaw at our vitals. Our own intellectual progress is the very thing that now destroys us.

We are obliged to go forward, to press onwards to the unknown future, not merely to retrace regressively our footsteps to the forgotten past. What we have gained so laboriously in these many centuries of evolution we cannot sacrifice without deliberation, not even for God. And we cannot conceive that God would demand such abrogation of ourselves. That indeed would be disastrous and catastrophic. We would be untrue to our birthright. Instead, we must bring the past up-to-date, as it were. We must recover the former sense of our divine kinship with nature, with things, with men. Then we can press forward, taking with us what we have formerly gained from nature by dint of heroic effort and struggle and experiment.

By adding the past, with its volcanic power and creative force, to the present of reason and logical judgment, a superior combination will have been effected. A true whole will have its problems, but every level, every faculty of the whole mind, the whole self, were enlisted in one prodigious effort. In his book *The Integration of the Personality*, Jung devotes a whole chapter to the analysis of numerous dreams of a single person, pointing out how the primordial archetypes were evoked into redemptive activity to bring about this desired process of integration, the achievement of wholeness, of perfection.

Possibly one great advantage of the psalms and ancient prayers or invocations lies in the fact that they awaken memories, not merely of infancy but of the far distant past. They bring us in touch once more with the unconscious self hidden deep in our own minds. Therefore, we impinge upon the whole collective background of our individual lives, upon the immeasurable past of duration when the instinctual forces—symbols of powers of miraculous potency and superior wisdom—flourished and prospered and functioned without the conscious interference that belongs to our present day and age. Through such usage of prayer, we recover the vitality and in the involuntary higher guidance that obtains in the acquisition of the knowledge of our instincts. Moreover, and what is important for us, we obtain the sense of participating with and belonging to the whole rhythmic stream of life which pulses and vibrates in the world around us.

One of the most outstanding characteristics of primitive man was *participation mystique*, an anthropological term to denote that mystical sense of identification with nature, when trees and rivers and clouds, and every phenomenon soever, were alive and spoke. Nature was intelligent and peopled widely with dryads and hamadryads, with nympths, fauns and centaurs. This, today, we would call the projection of unconscious images, the projection as on to an outer mirror of the world of what actually existed within. Primitive man projected their own primitive know in the least the *modus operandi* of suggestion, yet a similar comment can be made upon prayer. We have not the least knowledge how prayer, when successful, operates and how it produces the amazing results which occasionally we do see. For the sake of convenience therefore, we could use the word suggestion and auto-suggestion possibly, in order to convey the same series of ideas as are involved in the idea of prayer.

Moreover, for the sake our own understanding, we can liken the process of successful evocation of inner states of consciousness by means of prayer, which overcomes resistance at the gates of the unconscious levels, by reference to Jungian analysis. The contemplation of dreams in the light of mythological and religo-philosophical processes, awakens out of their latency primordial archetypes that are residues of former cultural periods, to function anew within the conscious sphere. These residues are the psychological imprints, as it were, left by the efforts of former generations of men to solve satisfactorily their own inner and spiritual problems.

As we ourselves become confronted by difficulties of mind and emotion with which we do not know how to deal, the libido, or the mind's energy, under the stimulus of analysis slips away or regresses from the present time into the past. It regresses not merely to infancy, but to older and more ancient levels within the mind where are stored the phylogenetic results of man's age-old attempts adequately to fulfill ourselves and our spiritual aspirations. These historical records or primordial archetypes of the collective unconscious often assume in dreams the guise of magical processes of old, formerly celebrated religious rites, mythological worship and devotions paid to the old gods. These archetypes, layer by layer, become successively awakened by means of the analytical process. It is as though not merely superficial aspects of the mind labored to deal with duration—to permit of the immediate acceptance of the suggestions. Once in the mind's deeper structure, they can do their work effectively. From within they evoke various states of consciousness that are constantly present though dormant. They are rather like parental imagos present within the unconscious levels of the mind, remaining dormant until mobilized or reinforced by current events or people. The dormancy is overcome by the prayer, and these latent psychic states are stimulated sympathetically into dynamic activity by the suggestions. Suggestions by themselves mean nothing, and of themselves contribute nothing. They only render kinetic previous but unknown contents of the mind.

I am quite willing to admit calling this process suggestion or auto-suggestion does not in the least render explicable to our minds what we know to occur. A psychological phenomenon of extraordinary interest and power has occurred. We do not know what it really is, but we give it the name suggestion. Merely to give a scientific term to an unknown process, however, does not necessarily explain it—though this seems to be a common trait of the modern scientific and critical mind. Nor do these terms tell us in what way suggestion works, nor the inner mechanism of its operation within the mind itself. But at least this may be said. The phenomena of suggestion to some extent can be experimentally induced—presuming that we have a good subject and a capable operator—and that goes a very long way for us. This is more than can be said of prayer in its formal religious or even metaphysical sense. I have never heard of any metaphysician who would be willing to "demonstrate" under test conditions. But this is exactly what can be done with suggestion and auto-suggestion. Very severe scientific conditions have been imposed upon experimenters, and these have been satisfactorily fulfilled. And though we do not averse to conceiving of prayer as a complex process of auto-suggestion. The so-called affirmations of modern metaphysics are quite obviously suggestions. One ancient prayer, or invocation, as once they were called, strongly and frequently employs in its structure the modern usage of "I am" affirmations. For example, it affirms as part of its rubic, "I am He the Bornless Spirit having sight in the feet, strong, and the immortal fire. I am He the Truth. I am He whose mouth ever flameth. I am He that lighteneth and thundereth. I am He from whom is the shower of the Life of Earth. I am He the Grace of the World."

This is the peroration of a long and complicated prayer filled with certain obscure and barbaric elements not altogether comprehensible to the modern mind. There is little doubt however but that the motivating trend of the preliminary parts of the prayer or invocation was gradually to excite the so-called conscious mind of the invoker until a high pitch of fervour was induced. It affirmed the relationship of man to God, narrating the great power and wisdom of God. The intention was that the mind at the critical moment, due to the extraordinary degree of excitement and ardor provoked, should be thrown into a state of high suggestibility. That arden peak achieved, the peroration containing the potent suggestions was uttered, and the magical results were obtained because the suggestions were accepted and became effectual.

A state of high suggestibility is one during which the normal reticence of the mind to extraneous ideas, the endo-psychic resistance of which psychoanalysis speaks, is overcome. This overcoming of the resistance may be not necessarily be a permanent conquest. But from the point of view of the prayer technique, that is a matter of very small moment. The resistance is abrogated for a sufficiently long period—a few seconds or a few minutes at most may be its one topic, and a total concentration of his mind on that single topic procured. It is for this reason, then, that emotional exaltation is so necessary to metaphysical technique, or to the practice of auto-suggestion, for then the mind's stream becomes automatically narrowed down to a single point, permitting the penetration of the suggestion.

We must pray so the whole being becomes aflame with a spiritual devotion, before which nothing can stand. In that intensity, we rediscover what we always have been in reality. All illusions and errors and limitations fade utterly away before this divine fervor. When the soul literally burns up—"as pants the hart for cooling stream," as the popular hymn goes—then spiritual identity with, or realization of, God becomes more than a possibility. "The desire of Thy house hath burnt me up." Then the heart's desire is accomplished without effort—because actually it is God who prays and God who answers. There is none other to pray, and nothing that can be accomplished, save that for which God makes the gesture. The desire that is holy becomes fact—objective phenomenal fact for all to see.

Prayer is a dramatic gesture, implying the utmost in emotional capacity and in spiritual understanding. It bears no relationship to the infantile concept of asking favors of some father-like deity. It is, however, a gesture of realizing the divine reality that has never been obscured, save in the conscious mind. Unconsciously we have always known what we were and to what spiritual power we were related. That knowledge has never been entirely lost. By making gestures of the right and most intelligent kind, we regain a full and conscious realization of our own Godhead.

A study of ancient prayer techniques seems to yield the fact that former authorities, unlike so many today, were not in demonstration comes about not exclusively through human effort, but primarily because the divine force courses through one. First, however, one must have touched adequately the divine universal mind, and right rapture provides the drive towards that goal.

I have always questioned in my mind whether prayer of the quiet unemotional variety is of any ultimate value at all. This cold blooded petitioning finds no real place within the highest conceptions of spiritual achievement. An ancient mystic and metaphysician once wrote we should *inflame* ourselves with prayer. And here is the secret revealed in a single word. We must not, counsels Jesus, use vain repetitions as the heathens do. But we may repeat intelligently the prayer again and again until the meaning is driven home, firing us spontaneously to increased devotion.

In his fascinating book *The Psychology of Suggestion*, Dr. Boris Sidis made an observation which is particularly apropos and pertinent to this discussion. He remarks, "we know that a strange emotion narrows down the field of consciousness." In this way, therefore, suggestions are much more readily accepted by the subconscious mind, than were the mind extensive and preoccupied with a host of sensory perceptions and motor impulses. "We often find," he continues, "that people under the emotion of intense excitement lose, so to say, their senses; their mind seems to be paralyzed, or rather, so to say, the one idea that produces the excitement banishes all other ideas, and a state of monoideism, or concentration of the consciousness is thus effected." Monoideism was the term employed by [Dr. James] Braid\* to describe the hypnotic state, when the subject's attention, all plastic and pliable, could be turned to any

---

\* Dr. James Braid was a Scottish surgeon, often considered the father of modern hypnosis.

whole secret of prayer lies in this direction. It aims at ecstatically moving the individual to transcend themselves. In short, prayer consists of a complex of psychological gestures designed to enable us to recover our true identity—which is God. In praying, we evolve to the stature of full and perfect adulthood, where we are able to perceive our true and essential relationship to all that lives, and our entire dependence upon the One Mind in whom we do exist and have our being.

Not only is this an intellectual or mental achievement, but the realization itself becomes fired by the rapture that the meditation on prayer should arouse. As a successful operation, prayer must provide scope for man's every faculty. Thus conceived, it is the spiritual and emotional stimulus that is calculated to restore the sense of our original identity with Godhead. Or, at least, it will enable the individual to contact in some novel and dynamic way that boundless source of power and wisdom which we conceive of as God. It is no request to an impossible God for bounty or reward like a child asking presents of its mother or father. Sincerely undertaken, prayer should mobilize all the qualities of the self. Integrity is the essence and goal of its nature. The inner fervor it awakens should reinforce the whole individual, energizing the concept s/he holds in mind for treatment so it becomes realized as concrete reality. This inner fervor is the *sine qua non* of success.

Neville [Goddard] rightly surmises that to make one's prayers fulfill themselves one must go mad temporarily. Even as lovers become excited and moved by the fleeting thought of the sweetheart, so the one employing prayer should react also. They must be capable of becoming so enthused and spiritually excited by the prayer that the whole self lets go of itself and flies directly to its divine goal, as though impelled inexorably like an arrow from the bow of devotion and aspiration. Success

# ECSTACY

From Lucifer's Rebellion
by Israel Regardie
New Falcon Publications, Second Edition 2017

*[Note this is also the fifth chapter from Dr. Regardie's book Healing Energy, Prayer & Relaxation (New Falcon Publications).*
*Written later in his life, this book distills the knowledge he accumulated throughout a life of devoted study and practice in Magic, Natural Healing and Psychology.]*

An attitude of cold objectivity and lack of feeling during prayer is, so far as my understanding goes, quite impossible. I cannot conceive how a person who has pondered over the 23rd Psalm, for example, and understood it to the extent of employing it as their private and personal metaphysical treatment, can refrain from being moved emotionally. For a prayer to be successful it should have the effect of bringing about an inner crisis. Eventually it should induce a vigorous emotional reaction that, when understood and controlled and directed, can wing the soul towards the realization of the presence of God, the goal that is ever sought after. A real ecstasy should result, a thoroughgoing standing out of the mind from itself and all it concerns with the body and its problems, from neurosis and inner turmoils. It should raise the individual above their personality, so as to realize their true divine nature. The researchers gradually and laboriously confirming the age-old conclusions of the divine wisdom.

But a vast amount of work remains for those of us who are students of this wisdom. We must not rest on our hard-fought laurels, so to speak, and be content simply to accept the philosophy of the ancients on its own merits. We owe it both to ourselves and to mankind to make sure that we understand our inestimable heritage, and to study the advancing efforts of modern scientists and researchers in every field of endeavor, so that it will be within our power gently to call to them from no great distance and point to our philosophic possession. Comparison, classification and synthesis are urgently required, a great deal of work remaining yet to be performed in this direction.

psychologically, the father". To this, the Cabbalist would add the word "spiritually" also, for as we have seen, without that the process is hardly completed.

To sum up, then, because of certain cosmic activities and developments there are found within man what are called the Father and Mother complexes. The latter relates to the tendency on the part of the offspring to desire the tranquillity and power possessed not only in the physical womb, but in the unconscious Nirvana of Pralaya which preceded the Cycle of Manifestation. The other complex has reference to the indelible impress given to each constituent element of the created universe to become the creator. Not only physically so, which is the least important factor—though one, nevertheless, not to be ignored—but psychologically and spiritually so, by which is meant that that human principle which is active and spiritually creative must be allowed to make manifestation in the mind, heart and body that the purpose of life and incarnation may be fulfilled.

So, in the future, when we have hurled at us the facetious relegation of Mystical endeavor to queer complexes within the mind, we have only to answer "Agreed! But are you certain you understand the origin and the real implication of this Œdipus complex?" And it will be found in most cases that in retracing its influence the psychological amateur will stop short at a point in racial history, and refuse to go any further. And it is here, as it is in almost every branch of philosophy and knowledge, that Mysticism steps in with its ancient philosophy which has been checked and verified through countless æons, to unravel the twisted thread of human development, providing the key which will unlock the fast-closed door of mystery. It alone possesses the true psychology, although it is somewhat gratifying to find academic and independent constitute, with the Monad, the Higher Self. Air is the swift flowing, all penetrant, unstable, fluid power of the mind, the human ego which is the *Ruach*; and Earth represents the animal soul, the subconscious self which comprises the emotions, passions, instincts, and automatic impulses—the *Nephesch*. There is thus in man an active paternal principle and a passive maternal principle, the eidolons within him of cosmic processes and developments. The Cabbala proceeds yet further, and believes that human progress consists in the marriage of the Daughter with the Son, and in that mystical union consummated through the methods of Mysticism and Magic—a union wherein all conflicts and differences of personality are obliterated, harmonized, and merged together—the Daughter is set upon the Mother's throne, and the Son assumes the rôle of the Father. In this way, the animal soul submits itself as the handmaiden of the human soul, and the latter, discarding its complacency and worldly wisdom and false egoism, opens itself with love and devotion to the wisdom and intuitive rays of the Higher Self.

It is for man to continue in the cosmic tradition which inheres in the flesh of his body and in the soul of his spirit by virtue of the recapitulation process, if he is to be biologically sound. He must take the place of his paternal parent, by fulfilling his own duty and becoming the father of his own family. This is so far as concerns the physical side alone. Psychologically, he must shake off the enmity and egoic rivalry with the father through the realization that he, in turn, has become invested with paternal gifts through arriving at physical maturity and possesses the magical power. In Dr. Howe's book mentioned above, it is stated as axiomatic "that the goal of wish-fulfilment for the son is to become, biologically and

The psycho-pathologies of the *imagos*, however, must be left for consideration to others more competent than myself; it is only the general trend and nature of the conception which claims my attention.

First, we see the male, vigorous cosmic force and power—the Father as it were of all life, alone, without rival or equal, all-powerful, and mighty—which fructifies the passive female element in the universe awaiting the germ of life that will make of her the pregnant Mother, *Aimah* of the Zohar, and thus the first nebuæ are germinated. Repeating itself on a lower, more dense metaphysical plane in the formation of a particular solar system within the limitless bounds of the cosmos, the identical process continues with the positing of a laya centre and the development of the globes of a planetary chain, the entire impetus culminating as a propelling force in racial history, represented to-day, among other things, in man's subconscious attitude towards his father.

Inasmuch as that which proceeds universally has its correlatives within the sphere of mankind, the larger cycles reproducing themselves in lesser cycles, the Cabbala postulates that these four elements of the Tetragrammaton inhere likewise within the constitution of man. In fact, the Tetragrammaton formula is peculiarly useful as the type and symbol of man. As above, so below. Man in this particular scheme is a fourfold being crowned by the flame of the Spirit, the divine Monad which transcends and directs the other principles, corresponding in the Macrocosm to the Ancient of Days. There is Fire, man's spiritual soul of creative Will and Wisdom—called the *Chiah*; Water his divine soul on the passive side, including intuition, understanding and love—the *Neschamah*; these two principles the Daughter. Thus the complex processes of the evolution of the Universe, in all its heterogeneous aspects and multiform ramifications, are familiarly and eloquently conceived under the guise of domestic relationship. For the union of the primal elements, cosmic fire and water—or, as Blavatsky names them, Cosmic Ideation and Root-substance, the Father and Mother respectively—gives birth to lesser elements and other planes of substance, comprehended under the symbolism of the Son and Daughter, Air and Earth. From this association of four elements and their subsequent union and interaction proceed all manifested things and beings.

Thus, to anticipate a little, the rivalry and intense jealousy in the primitive tribe as to who among the youths should succeed to the patriarchy was not, in reality, the ultimate traceable cause of the father-imago. Actually but the expression of an inner urge to power, this rivalry was a dynamic impetus recapitulated from a vast cosmic process propelling man forward to claim his rightful place as the patriarch of his race, the chief parent of his family, and the father of himself. What is required as Jung so well expressed it, is the domestication of the libido or the *élan vital*, the harnessing of these great cosmic and spiritual forces which course in our minds and even in our blood to the work and problems of conventional civilized life. Within the soul, latent, are tremendous powers which but seldom are given the opportunity to work openly. Only a fraction of them are manifested. And these, if ever they do succeed in penetrating the mind and heart of man, are prevented in their direct expression and turned aside from their true course by centuries of false notions of convention, repression and ignorance of their true divine nature. Thus they manifest in numbers of cases as neuroses.

has become thwarted, and then mixed up with all sorts of animal impulses in which the perverse idea of incest plays a prominent rôle. But this properly belongs to psychoanalysis and its proper form of therapeutics with which I am just now concerned. The complex as known to many moderns is but a distortion, a perversion of a really divine urge—distorted because its underlying truth is unrecognized; perverted because deliberately repressed—the urge to seek not merely the physical womb, but our divine heritage and place of birth with the spiritual gifts of our earthly sublunary experience.

There is yet another mode of consideration which may throw considerable amplification on the nature of the Mother-Father complex, using the so-called Formula of Tetragrammaton, which figures a great deal in Cabbalistic exegesis. It is conceived that from the first manifestation which is named the Ancient of Days, appearing within the infinity of *Ain Soph*, flow forth in powerful waves of activity the four cosmic elements, four distinct surges of vitality, life and power. The Ancient of Days is the dimensionless Point of concentrated Light, the First Cause and the unmanifested Logos from whose latent homogeneity both Spirit and Matter are subsequently differentiated. The four noumenal elements are Fire, Water, Air and Earth—not the terrestrial elements we normally cognize as such, but the soul, as it were, of all of these on a plane of metaphysical abstraction. To each is attributed a letter of the Tetragrammaton—YHVH; and in The Book of Splendour, further symbols of a most recondite and profound nature are associated with the letters and elements of the Tetragrammaton. Y, Fire, is named the Father; H, primal, Water, is conceived to be the Mother; V, Air, is the Son; and the final H, Earth, is

I do not wish to be so misunderstood as to countenance a return to anthropomorphic views, but I feel that there is no uncertain authority for the employment of this interpretation. From a philosophical, that is rational, point of view, I fully recognize that such an idea may seem childish and certainly naive, but that does not necessarily invalidate the essential *suggestiveness* of the idea. In point of fact, memory recalls a passage in the *Zohar* where, with gracious poetry and phantasy, it is described how the spirits of men were gathered before the throne of the Ancient of Ancients prior to being sent down to earth where they were to incarnate, and in that heavenly condition on high they expressed their unwillingness to be divided from their celestial sources of nourishment and sustenance, and to leave the divine womb. If this be assumed as working hypothesis, that the Gods or the divine Cosmic forces which first issued from the Infinite Unmanifest at the early blush of the golden dawn so with a sort of unwillingness or reluctance—also corroborated by the dynamic tendency inhering in all forces to return to a state of inertia, the primal condition of things—then every intelligence and entity developed or projected from within the essence of those high Gods would likewise be impressed with that universal Œdipus complex, if so it may be called. The whole universe would be permeated with the desire to return to the Source of Life, for That alone can bestow peace, serenity, and bliss. With the philosophic theory of recapitulation, this tendency would be repeated, though in a lesser degree, and the cosmic endeavour to return by evolution to the primeval inertia would show forth in the unconscious desire of the child to return as the psychologists put it, to the womb of its Mother. I am, of course, aware of instances where the primary spiritual instinct as the spiritual source where from all created things have issued, and to which at the close of the great cycle of manifestation, they will eventually be withdrawn. On various of the Egyptian sacerdotal stélés and papyri are vignettes and representations of the form of a Woman whose body is so arched that her hands and feet, touching the world at different points, enclose within a limited finite area, all things and all beings. This female form is the goddess Nuit, representing in the poetry of the ancient Egyptian cosmogony the omnipresence of Space and Infinity, and of her it is most picturesquely said that the Stars and the milk of the stars issue from her breasts. She corresponds in a unique way to the Cabbalistic idea of the impersonal *Ain Soph*, from whom the Universe with its Ten Sephiros or categories of creative thought evolved. Nuit is the cosmic Mother, as it were, who gave birth to stars, nebulæ, suns, planets, angels, spirits, and all sublunary creatures from her own divine essence—the Mother of each one of us, although so far removed from our normal conceptions and speculative efforts as to be well-nigh incomprehensible and unknown to us, her children. I wonder whether it would be stretching philosophical probability too far to suggest that the first cosmic manifestations, the supernal Dhyan Chohanic forces, issuing from Her interior life with as much reluctance as does a child from the womb of its mother, bore within them an indelible impress of their spiritual origin, an innate yearning for the restoration of their primeval Nirvana, a craving which communicated itself to all the products of their ideation. Before manifestation they were part and parcel of the celestial body of the Mother, a unity in which no trace of imperfection marred the absolute peace, power, and serenity of that life. Within the being of Nuit all was bliss and joy, but with the opening of the cycle of the Day ensued duality—the great curse; and with it deprivation, struggle, and difficulty.

all modern occult philosophers of any consequences: Blavatsky, Steiner, Heindl—will be found the means of at last providing a suitable explanation for the existence in the mind of civilized mankind of the Mother-Father complex, and reconciling the ancient and modern systems of thought. First of all, I feel that modern psychology has committed a definite mistake in limiting the theory of recapitulation to *racial* experience alone. This probably is the root from which misunderstanding has grown. Occult Philosophy is one where the concept of evolution is not only fully recognized, but expanded in a highly comprehensive scheme of cosmic and universal development which, naturally, recapitulates itself in the evolution and progress of the human being. "As above, so below" is an aphorism of the esoteric philosophy which, because of so frequent reiteration, sometimes loses force when we do not attend sufficiently closely to its implication. Man also, it is said, is the Microcosm of the Macrocosm—another well-worn phrase, but one nonetheless true and none the less worthy of constant repetition because of its familiarity. The Sephiros and spiritual regions which are evolved in the course of the manifestation of a Cosmos are, by analogy, also represented and mirrored forth in the constitution of man, and whatever major processes are operated in the universe repeat or recapitulate themselves on a lesser scale and in a minor way in the Sephiros inhering within the individual being. Occult theories of evolution are perhaps too well known to the readers of the OCCULT REVIEW to necessitate their repetition at any great length here, but in order to develop this reconciliation thesis I propose mentioning the principal ideas involved in the Cabbalistic emanation theory.

The mediæval doctors of the Cabbala—more poets and mystics than philosophers—conceived of Infinite Space, *Ain Soph*,

The repression of these impulses tends to imbed them in the subconsciousness, where, apart from any actual psychic disturbance of equilibrium, they modify and direct for instance our personal reactions to such worldly matters as politics, economics, religion, and domestic relation.

Prior to turning these psychological conceptions to a discussion of how to achieve a reconciliation with the esoteric philosophy, it is necessary to consider one more orthodox theories—that of Recapitulation. By this term is understood that process by which an individual life repeats a line of development representing a sum of previous racial experiences. The best example which readily occurs to mind is that which takes place in the development of the fœtus *in utero*, where it passes in a brief span of time through all those stages of evolution and development which have marked the biological progress of the human race in its forward surge. Recapitulation implies a speeding up of the time factor, so to speak, during which the experience of many thousands, perhaps millions, of years is repeated in the individual, both *intra-* and *extra-utero*. Anatomically and psychologically, the individual is himself but the apex of a vast pyramid, the base of which is formed by ancient history—racial and cosmic. The basis of the academic theory of the two complexes just outlined and the ideology of Recapitulation may be consulted to great advantage in some such work as *Motives and Mechanisms of the Mind*, by E. Graham Howe, *Lancet*, 1931.

It is in this theory of Recapitulation, I think, that the clue to a valuable comparison between Occult Philosophy and modern Psychology must be sought. I believe that in this theme—also developed and expanded though along different lines by nearly patriarch was installed in his stead. The two outstanding points which compel interest, are the rivalry between the patriarch and the youthful competitors, and the rivalry amongst those desiring to become the patriarch, and this conception of a recapitulation of unconscious rivalry adds to our knowledge and understanding of adolescent development. On the one hand, preventing the complete enjoyment or possession of the mother stands the father, possessed of knowledge and power acquired through the status of his years. On the other, the growing sons whose developing urge towards the fulfilment of their lives lead them to regard the father with criticism and frank disapproval. This, manifestly, has it basis in previous racial experience, the desire of the youth for the patriarchal post. In short, this unconscious rivalry, the Father imago, is firmly rooted in each one of us, and like the Mother complex as I hope to show, it is something greater and deeper than the mere disapproval of the actual father; it may be independent of him and the reality of personal father experience.

We have here then two complexes which, state the psychologists, determine the course of our ordinary intellectual life; the unconscious rivalry with and disapproval of the father, the innate urge demanding the imperative fulfilment of our needs and the attainment of relative omnipotence, and the desire for the apron strings of the mother, who, we subconsciously feel, is still capable of gratifying our every wish. Between the mother and the fulfilment of this desire stands the Father. These complexes, certainly not pleasant ideas to face when unprepared in childhood or adolescence, are universally regarded with horror and loathing, and when they do enter the realm of consciousness are as hastily thrust out and repressed forthwith.

human limitations, endeavouring to fulfil or attain to our infantile conception of undifferentiated ego and effortless omnipotence. Hence, the desire for a larger spiritual life, the aspiration to unify the individual human soul with a more comprehensive transcendental source of wisdom, bliss, and spirituality—whether that be conceived of a God or as Higher Self—upon which in time of adversity one may unhesitatingly lean, has certain quite distinct parallels to the desire for the peace and comparative omnipotence which one enjoyed *in utero;* this is the Œdipus complex. In each man, claims the psychologist, lurks the desire to possess or be possessed by his mother, for she is rest, fulfilment, and safety.

The other complex, second only in importance and significance to the Œdipus complex, is the Father-feeling or *imago*. Although for the sake of convenience father and mother *imagos* have been divided, it will be seen that they are in fact interdependent, the one being closely associated with complementary feelings about the other. An understanding of this demands reference to early tribal conditions in a former stage of evolution. The primitive tribal unit then was held together by the tribal chief or patriarch, who was in a very real sense the head and owner of the tribal family. The patriarch possessed supreme rights over the members and property of the tribe, holding undisputed sway until such time as he was no longer able to maintain it by forces of physical strength. It is easy to imagine that his authority was maintained only in the face of considerable resistance on the part of the stronger and younger members of the tribe. As the patriarch grew old and feeble, the power of his rule inevitably diminished and the criticism of those youths who wished to replace him grew stronger. Eventually, either the patriarch died or was removed, and after a certain amount of quarrelling amongst the rival sons for the leadership, a new brilliantly conveyed by Dion Fortune in *Psychic Self-Defence*, where a remark closing the paragraph is "the Rabbis knew their psychology". It is because I also feel that the Rabbis knew their psychology, and did understand so well the working of the human mind, that I venture to restate one or two of their theorems side by side with those of present-day savants in order that the subtleties of the Cabbala in both its philosophical and practical aspects may better be appreciated. Freud's hypothesis, then, is certainly true in a large proportion of mankind, as his own voluminous records undoubtedly testify, but it cannot and does not apply to humanity as a whole.

Having thus summarily disposed of Freud, let us turn our attention to the so-called Mother Complex which will be considered as a general psychological theory shorn of all specific pathologies. Briefly, this may be outlined in the following manner. Psychologists consider that before physical birth, the state of a baby must as nearly approach Nirvana in its feelings of peace, placidity, and omnipotence, as it is possible for any human to conceive, because its every need is supplied immediately without effort on its own part, and it is protected from external shock and danger. There can be little doubt that the more or less sudden change from the intrauterine life of complete tranquility to the different exterior world must come as a rude shock or awakening, and life in the vale of tears commences as a sequence of effort, struggle, and deprivation. In the beginning of physical existence there is no essential difference between the mother and child; the one is part and parcel of the other. Even after birth, the mother exists as a constant and faithful source of gratification of the infant's hunger, and as the fulfilment of its every need. For the rest of our lives, then, it may be said that we struggle against our region, from step to step. During the ascent she comes in contact with impure spirits who lie in wait for her at the entrance to the upper regions. If the soul herself is pure, she rises above the power of these spirits and continues her upward flight. But if her tendency is to be impure, she is powerless to go on, remaining the whole night in the company of the powers of Evil." (Bension's *Zohar*, p. 141.)

This particular rationale, however, does not apply universally, for "the souls of those who have not misused their bodies *can* rise without effort above the importunities of evil spirits". The Freudian hypothesis of a sexual dream interpretation is robbed of absolute application by the fact that numerous individuals, consciously or otherwise, have the various constituents of their being under some degree of control, so that there is no *Nepheschic* disturbance to hinder them passing through the dream-state of *Yesod* into a deep slumber, during which consciousness again centres in *Tipharas*—the proof being absolute refreshment and re-energization upon waking.

With regard to the above quotation from the Zohar it is necessary to remind the reader that "Angels", "Spirits", and "Powers" of the Practical Cabbala and Magic are, by one definition, "ideas" of varying degrees of power, sublimity, and significance which exist and function unperceived in the different regions of our subliminal consciousness. Hence the evil spirits referred to are, perhaps, impure memories of the day stored in the Subconscious which, together with the repressed desires and animal impulses—the "power of evil"—tend to delay the passage of the consciousness to a purer state or condition by the ghoulish symbols of sexuality which the *Ruach*, the conscious self, refuses to face in their stark reality. Very much the same *rationale* underlying the neurotic dream experience is universal application and validity. In this connection one can only remind both groups of the extraordinary clarity thrown on this problem by the diagrammatic Tree of Life and the fundamentals of the doctrinal Cabbala. The latter assumes that during sleep, consciousness ceases to focus within the physical brain, and tends to ascend to its own plane, which in the Cabbala is the central Sephirah of *Tipharas*. (see charts 4 and 8 in *A Golden Pomegranates*.) In the process of ascent it must of necessity pass through the Sephirah of *Yesod*—the Foundation—described in the *Sepher ha Zohar* in such a manner as to indicate its sexual character, thus pointing to an important correspondence with the academic idea of the Subconscious. The theory is that when a more or less profligate life has been consistently followed, or one perhaps in which undue attention was given to sexual and emotional matters, the Sephirah of *Yesod*, as well as its human representative the *Nephesch*, is thrown into a violent state of inequilibrium and disordered activity, which results in a dream-life typified by a wealth and chaos of lurid symbolism of dubious connotation, preventing the consciousness returning as it were to its own plane.

"Our soul longs for God during the night, and our spirit seeks for God from the break of day. When man sleeps, his soul leaves him and ascends to the upper world. But not all the souls are able to come into the presence of the Heavenly King. When the soul leaves the body she leaves behind her shadow (that is, the substantive aspect of *Nephesch*—the astral body) in order to keep life in the body,* while she rises from region to

---

* One is tempted to break a lance on the battlefield of occult misconceptions. The above quotation is distinctly in opposition to the teaching of those neo-theosophic schools which hold that in sleep the astral body wanders aimlessly outside the physical body. The Zohar corroborates Blavatsky's teaching that in all but a few cases the astral body does not leave its physical double during the latter's sleep.

is the perfect medium not only for classification, but alike for comparison and synthesis.

Some mention first of all must be made of the Freud dream-psychology before we can dispose of the more complex Mother and Father imagos. Briefly, the Freudian hypothesis postulates that underlying our waking consciousness functions a dynamic stream of dionysian energy, emotion, and memory of previous racial experience, the sensuous dictates of which we, who live in an enclosed civilized society wherein we are obliged to set a curb to primitive passional expression, find it necessary to repress. Inasmuch as the vast majority of us refuse consciously to attend to this dynamic urge to a more complete physical life, a brilliant and seductive pageant of sexual impulse well-shrouded in archaic symbol is presented to the individual during the hours of sleep in the fantastic adventure of dream—that is, when the latter is obviously not traceable to such physical causes as indigestion, toxaemia, and so forth, or to the stress of memory generated by the day's events and happenings. Unfortunately, on the one hand, many mystically-minded philosophers who should know better have denominated Freud and the Freudian practitioners as "dirty-minded schoolboys". This opprobrium is absurd and distinctly unfair, since for one thing no fact however seemingly "dirty" must be ignored in scientific research, and moreover because Freud was a pioneer in the realm of the mind, the first to introduce into the world Psychology the concepts of meaning, purpose and motive. On the other hand, while responsible for an immense amount of good in breaking down the moulds of men's minds and in having helped to destroy sex taboos and false notions of bourgeois convention, Freud has gyrated to the opposite pole, considering his hypothesis as of his philosophical scheme, and since he is unable to reconcile the two, he experiences the reckless inclination to reject the whole concatenation of observed and clinically verified facts upon which a large part of the structure of modern psychology has reared itself. Rather than discard his Mysticism, or even seek a clearer understanding of his beliefs, a wholesale rejection is resorted to. Likewise, the devoted student of modern analytical methods and ideas, finding himself unable to discover in the works of accredited mystics and occult writers parallels with his own accumulated data, flies to the other extreme, and discards their contributions as having no intrinsic value—ambiguous phantasies of wish-fulfilment.

Yet both these conventional attitudes are erroneous, for the writer believes that the moderns, step by step, are approaching that psycho-spiritual edifice constructed by the ancient philosophers, and to which the name Mysticism may be given. To be quite truthful, however, even with the deepest erudition one cannot produce an *exact* comparison, inasmuch as even now science and psychology have far to go before catching up with the broad outlines of mystical philosophy. The essential difference in all probability between mystical and academic research is this: Mysticism has ever sought the universal, the broad generalization, whereas Psychology and Western science as a whole have occupied themselves with the detailed and the particular. Those particulars *must* fit in with the universals—else one or the other is inaccurately stated. When attempting, therefore, the difficult task of comparison, a knowledge of the Cabbala is practically indispensable, since the fundamental basis of the Cabbala—the Tree of Life, with its Ten Sephiros, amplified by a host of significant correspondences of ideas, symbols, and numbers—

# ASPIRATION AND THE "MOTHER COMPLEX"

By Israel Regardie
New Falcon Publications, First Edition 2017
Originally from The Occult Review, Rider & Co., March, 1933

Of all the perplexing problems confronting to-day the earnest student of Mysticism—that is, one who entertains the aspiration, and cherishes the ideal dearly beyond all others, that of Divine Union—the most disconcerting is the glib statement reiterated by the psychological amateur that "Mysticism simply has its origin in the Œdipus complex!" Such an ethical injunction in the *Light on the Path* as "Look for the Warrior, and let him fight in thee...he is eternal and is sure," and some such phrase as "the worlds of rest eternal" in Blavatsky's *Voice of the Silence* are brusquely dismissed as indicative of little else but unconscious yearnings for the peace and power of the mother's womb. In the large majority of cases, needless to say, the individual making such a rash statement is wholly under fully explains the mysterious baggage to which that label is attached. *Vox et praterea nihil*. No such folly is indulged in by the well-informed practising psychologist. The average student of Occult philosophy is ofttimes puzzled, nevertheless, by this apparently psychological explanation of his innermost desire, for he believes that the obscure rationale of the Mother Complex nowhere appears in we trespass into the medical field, or to use forbidden drugs which, in the last resort, merely mask and distort the basic organismic disturbance. The current chiropractic armamentarium is enhanced and broadened by the inclusion of vegeto-therapy within its own framework. It is naturalistic, biological, and at the same time spiritual in its orientation because its last court of appeal is not faith but experience. In any case, it seems to me that balanced living, a life of understanding and spiritual experience, a life of creativity and spontaneity and inner growth is made possible by this happy combination of therapies.

whole areas of society forcing them to erect unnatural moral barricades and absurd rationalizations against all healthy natural processes. And if you want to obtain still another glimpse of what the plague is like universally, read the biographical-novel of *Citizen Thomas Paine* by Howard Fast. If your heart does not bleed then, indeed you must be very heavily armored.

Someone has said facetiously that by orgastic potency Reich meant a bigger and better orgasm. Facetious or not, and however ludicrous it may seem, one of the principle outcomes of good psychotherapy must be a considerable improvement in the sexual function. But Reich differentiated carefully between erective potency and orgastic potency. It is the difference between lack of sexual gratification even though pursuing what appears to be an active sex life, and the total orgastic satisfaction eventuating in optimal physical health and the highest kind of mental and spiritual creativity. It is the difference between physical rigidity and tension even after coitus, and the total bodily and mental release. It is the difference between unsatisfied promiscuity, and a happy fidelity based on mutual satisfaction, love, and respect. It is the difference between compulsive function and healthy naturalness. To this extent, this sexual outlook is rendered far more "moral" than any hidebound, compulsive, moralistic philosophy of today. Reich's book, *The Function of the Orgasm* discusses this at considerable length together with the whole concept of vegeto-therapy and other psychological matters.

Each one of these significant topics requires a whole volume for further elucidation. Many of these ideas may seem to some students altogether foreign, but to others they will fall on ready soil. These topics and the method of vegeto-therapy provide the missing link to chiropractic, and enable us to forge a successful chiropractic psychotherapy. It does not require that

5. Subsequent research became summarized under the initials C.O.R.E.—cosmic orgone engineering. This began a few years before his untimely death in 1957 with an investigation into the possible use of the orgone accumulator as an antidote to destructive atomic radiation. His findings were so encouraging as to lead to speculations about "smog," weather in general, storm-control, drought and desert conditions. From all this, there emerged a tentative technique for the production of rain in arid areas of the country. Whether or not there is any validity to this kind of speculative activity, I personally do not know. I do know, though, that ridicule is such a stupid answer to a great man's creativity. Objective research and patient investigation would be a far more telling answer. Admittedly this is a far cry from the treatment of psychoneurosis. But as one friend has reminded me, Leonardo's monoplane notes were also a far cry from the Mona Lisa!

Another factor which he stressed in connection with the achievement and maintenance of psychosomatic well-being was the sexual factor. He believed that sexual inhibition based upon our irrational social and religious more had a great deal to do not only with cancer and neurosis but with the growth of the *emotional plague*. By this latter term he meant a chronic biopathy of crippling outlook on social living. Psychoanalytically, it could be considered the outcome first of repression—with reaction-formation, displacement, identification and projection added to the imposing list of defense mechanisms, forming a species of paranoid attitude towards everything and everybody. And this psychopathological attitude remains localized not within a single individual but tends to spread in the immanent group until it reaches epidemic proportions. A history of chiropractic gives ample evidence of the viciousness of plague reactions. It becomes a diseased psychic attitude which infects man's finding his proper place in a dynamic universe. It results in the emergence of a naturalistic-religious attitude from the former psychoanalytical approach that had been so thoroughly iconoclastic. Much of this has been incorporated into his work *The Cancer Biopathy* which one day will be recognized as one of the world's greatest classics of medical literature.

This book also gives the results of some experimental evaluations of foodstuffs with regard to their orgone or vital content. His conclusions come remarkably close to those expounded by advocates of rational diet and organic foods. But he never fell into the cultist pitfall of assuming that a "rational diet" alone would cure many or all his physical and social ills, as do so many food fadists of today. Reich's background in psychoanalytical research and his former experiences relative to the socio-political origins of neurotic character-structure were much too intense for that.

Perhaps that part of his life-work which has evoked the most malicious and bitter medical criticism was related to his views about cancer. He came to relate cancer to rigid bodily areas which interfered with the natural flow of bioelectric energy and thus with good function, and psychic attitudes which were inhibitory to hostile feelings and full sexual gratification. Cancer, for him, was a matter of biological frustration, organismic shrinking, and psychological withdrawing. There would be no point describing the orgone accumulator in the first place, nor in summarizing at any length his views about cancer, for his own writings must be the final source of referral. Most of the venomous criticism, however, has been predicated on baseless prejudice and hate and medical monopolistic tyranny rather than on rational investigation. It may be some years before we can catch up with him to make some kind of restitution to his memory.

sickness, suffering and misery, and there was no complacency or compromise in him. His conversion to and subsequent rejection of communism netted him many bitter enemies who, even to this day, would prefer that his name and his work go down to oblivion. I believe this to be one of the major reason for his current ostracism by the scientific world, in addition to the two others—his sex-affirmativeness and his cancer theories.

4. In 1940, he expounded the existence of orgone radiation in the surrounding atmosphere and in the soil. The attempt to dissolve the muscular-character armor liberated not only emotions such as anger and anxiety and sex, but specific bioelectric energies which could be directly perceived proprioceptively by the patient as well-defined body sensations. When the technical therapeutic procedures induced a dynamic relaxation of muscular tension, that is to say when they had eliminated psychosomatic inhibition, there developed tingling sensations, clonisms, and other somatic phenomena in various regions of the body. Cautiously at first, but more emphatically later, Reich averred that these tingling and prickling sensations were caused by the free-flowing energies or orgone latent within the organism, energies which had been blocked in their motility by the chronic muscular tensions. When, by experimental work and not by mere intellectual speculation, he later found that these energies also existed external to man's own organism—in living, pulsating world of which he is intrinsically a part and with which he is in creative identity, whether he knows it or not—he formulated the view that there exists a cosmic stream of orgone energy. This is the basis and source of life. Such a theory also encourages an entirely new and more expressive attitude towards life and living. From the simple eradication of inner conflict and the dissolution of the muscular-character armor, the emphasis in therapy came to include within its province

"nonverbal psychotherapy." It represents the greatest single advance in psychological technique since the introduction of Freud's early "talking cure," to which most psychotherapy has remained stubbornly fixated. It made possible the first systematized attack against the grim problem of neurotic disease from the purely manipulative and somatic point of view. It enables us to use not only the traditional techniques of verbal communication in character analysis, but all forms of manipulation and adjustive techniques in a creative synthesis of therapeutic armaments.

One phase of the method bears some slight resemblance to so-called soft tissue manipulation. However, the motive is quite different. Here the goal is not merely to relax muscle and viscus but in so doing to release the inhibited affect. Successful manipulation of this type invariably results in the emergence of a vast series of affects. These include anxiety, rage, jealousy, sexual feelings, and resentment on the one hand, to weeping, love, pleasure, sympathy, etc., on the other. The patient recovers the long-lost sensitivity and sincerity of early childhood, characteristics of a healthy psyche that were submerged in the process of "growing-up," so-called.

Somewhere in this period, too, his psychological work and sex-teaching in clinics, exposed him to the mass-misery, poverty, and political inequities that he had not perceived earlier. As a result he threw himself enthusiastically into social and political reform in pre-war Germany. He became thereupon converted to communism. Arthur Koestler mentions him in *Darkness at Noon*. But his profound psychological insights could not let him rest content with being a mere Soviet sympathizer. So he rejected Red fascism just as totally as he had previously rejected Nazism and black Fascism. He was a sincere and outspoken student of life who was outraged by psychotherapy. Thus the therapeutic goal was the dissolution of neurotic character attitudes to permit a more spontaneous response to the ongoing, creative life-process.

3. The next period in his career was marked by the development of the concept of the muscular armor. By this phrase, he meant that the extensive development of muscular tensions or body rigidity served the same purpose as did the neurotic character structure. The armor served to repress inner feelings and instinctual drives, which training has labeled "bad" and "wicked," and to reduce the impact of the external world on a defensive organism. With this hypothesis, he concluded that the muscular armor and the character armor were functionally identical. The function of any chronic muscular tension is the inhibition of emotions and drives just as it is of the character armor. A retracted pelvis is as inhibitory of sexual drives as is a straightlaced moral attitude. An ever-present sweet smile, a chronically elevated stiff chest, and an apparently unruffled character can all serve the same biopsychological purpose—inhibition of angry impulses. Rigidity represents frozen emotion. Psychic rigidity enters bodily structure as generalized neuromuscular tension, visceral dysfunction, distorted posture and imbalance in body mechanics.

Not only invaluable to psychotherapy, the notion of the muscular-character armor throws a brilliant ray of light on many hitherto baffling problems in sociology, philosophy, ethics and religion. It resolves the paradox of the conflicting interests in man's single character structure. So far as chiropractic is concerned, the subluxation theory is considerably enhanced by the notion of the muscular armor.

The greater part of my present-day practice revolves around the use of these dynamics ideas and techniques which Reich called "vegeto-therapy." My more common phrase is minority, it amounted to an interference with Common Law and hence a violation of accumulated Common Sense."

Incidentally, it has always been a source of wonder to me that the lay public should address itself so trustingly for sexual counsel to the doctor—medical or chiropractic. The fact remains that apart from a short course in genesiology, the doctor's education contains little or nothing to fit him to be sex advisor. In fact, the well-educated layman is often better oriented in this regard than many a doctor who hides his sexual neurosis behind the framed diploma on the office wall.

2. In 1925, Reich indicated the possibility of the reductive analysis of neurotic character traits in much the same way as had previously been attempted with symptom analysis. This reached its logical conclusion in the publication of *Character Analysis*. Some of his findings and his dynamic approach were ridiculed by jealous colleagues and critics who were as vindictive towards him as they have been towards chiropractors. Today, however, the essential findings have been hailed as an important contribution and incorporated into the main body of psychoanalysis.

By "character" Reich called attention to the stereotyped *characteristic* way one had of responding to different life-situations. His viewpoint was that this rigid response was purposive, that it was wholly defensive in function. This kind of psychic control blocked off unacceptable feelings that welled up from within, serving at the same time to ward off frightening and hostile threats from the outside. It served as a psychic armor whose tragic sequel is the loss of spontaneity. Developing early in life, depending on the specific environment and psychological attitudes provided by the family, the character armor later becomes the causative factor in neurosis and the source of the major resistance to the successful progress of any form of to be made aware of its extraordinary validity and efficacy. For this reason, this scientist is of more than ordinary significance to our profession.

He was a dynamic thinker who, like Freud, was not averse to altering his pet theories when he found they no longer coincided with facts as he perceived them. This is certainly evidence of an open mind. It is also evidence that as the years progressed, he did too. For the sake of convenience, we can classify his lifework under five major headings:

1. That period prior to 1925 when he was an orthodox psychoanalyst. It is well known that he was, at the very least, a competent analyst. He lectured, taught and conducted clinics in Europe where he achieved a considerable reputation. Because of the specific orientation afforded by his psychoanalytic work, many of his lectures and clinics centered about sexual education. This he emphasized once he had discovered how little the general public or even the professional world knew about that topic which was so vital to their welfare and the ignorance about which was so often related causally to their abject misery and socio-economic impotence. This effort encountered, as you well may guess, a great deal of resistance from different vest interests in society. As Philip Wylie wrote in *An Essay on Morals*; "Sex...is the chief vested interest in religion. It is a principal concern of government. When the law and religion were embodied together in tribal custom, the administration of sex, next to traffic in ghosts, constituted the main means of continuum for those in authority. Machinations of tabu and privilege, unconscious and traditional though they were and usually still are, capture the libido (the psychic energies) of the many, and hold them subject to the authority of the few. Thus to most people, tampering with sex concepts was equivalent to tampering with the Laws of God, and to the more enlightened

## ON REICH
By Israel Regardie
New Falcon Publications, First Edition 2017

Until the recent advent of the miracle drugs, all forms of psychotherapy were drugless, revolving around the concept of verbalizing one's emotional difficulties. Insofar as "psyche" may be equated with the higher activities of the central nervous system, the methodology is in strict accord with the aims of chiropractic—the maintenance of the structural and functional integrity of the nervous system.

Because of this, it has always been a major source of disappointment to me that the profession has not more wholeheartedly exploited psychotherapy. About all it has done is to show some vague interest in hypnotism. Yet this has merely pandered to a desire for a thaumaturgical panacea, without contributing anything vital or dynamic to our knowledge of the psyche and its function.

Wilhelm Reich, one of the earliest disciples of Freud, has made so many contributions to psychotherapy that he has far outstripped the rank and file of the medical profession. There are some facets of his work, however, that bear many resemblances to chiropractic, or shall we say more accurately that his contribution fits chiropractic like tongue and groove. Adapting his work to the exigencies of the day provides us with a specific chiropractic psychiatry that only needs to be studied and experienced

the vile components of his repressed psyche. Moloney reminds one of a man who, upon marriage, pours forth a deluge of hate upon his mother-in-law, who in reality serves best as the embodiment of one phase of his emotional ambivalence to mother.

Moloney does not appear to realize that he has floundered into the very pitfall from which he is asked to extricate his patients. He complains that they surround themselves with a "magic cloak" of perfectionism. What else has he done here but to surround the medical profession with a magical cloak? Under this armouring, his profession can hide perfectly—or so he thinks. But he will not permit the chiropractor the luxury of the magic cloak. He will not permit the chiropractor to be of the same human stuff as the medical doctor—blessed with the same hopes, ideals, and visions, and cursed with the same infantile ineptness, traumata, and emotional blocks. Sometimes Maloney reverses the situation. The medical man is honest, good and scientific. Because he is so open and above-board, he does not require the magical cloak to cover his intellectual nudity. But the chiropractor is neither honest nor scientific, so therefore desperately needs the magical cloak of illusion to appear more than he is to the general public.

Maloney's book should be read. Every chiropractor specializing in the fields of psychiatry and psychotherapy should own it and read it. It should serve him as a guide and a model—of what to avoid. *Verbum sapienza.*

that I am not too well informed...Perhaps underlying my arguments may be many misconceptions and misunderstandings of chiropractic."

Well, this is honest. It is my general experience that the average psychiatrist who makes stupid generalizations about the chiropractor is poorly informed; nonetheless he has courage enough to recognize his mistake if he is approached on the psychiatric level. Whether Moloney is sufficiently honest for this remains to be seen.

In his book, discussing low back pains and the orthopedic surgeon, he admits the latter may be seduced by the patient's masochism, even that the latter may be narcissistic. He even goes so far as to admit that, lacking understanding of the psychosomatic problems involved, the orthopedic surgeon may attempt to get rid of the patient. He does not however attempt to berate the orthopedist for this infantile behavior. He leaves this venom for the chiropractor, who usually then gets this kind of patient. His comments about chiropractors indicate his own authoritarianism which he calls megalomania. Moloney says of the chiropractor: "He encourages," "he warns," "he threatens," he destroys effective "man-power," "he makes an impression upon anyone already 'sensitized' to the great dangers of success," etc.

Were Moloney and I discussing such language on the part of a prospective patient, we would be in complete agreement, I am sure, that the latter would be thoroughly paranoid. It reminds me of some of the late Julius Streichers' Nazi references to the Jew, which merely revealed Streichers' own sado-masochistic and paranoid trends relating to his own latent castration fears. Moloney, despite all his psychiatric insight, reveals his own paranoid trends, and his own castration fears. He needs the chiropractor to be the screen on which he can project all several others, fuming diatribes and vituperations against our inhuman practice of omitting emotional values from our therapeutic considerations. My viewpoint is fairly widely known as dogmatically insistent that we must incorporate some form of psychotherapy into chiropractic to leaven it, to lift it out of the unthinking chaos of decerebrate therapy. But I will have none of this neurotic idiocy on the part of those who theoretically should know better. I have waged and will continue to wage a relentless warfare on such people.

The quotations from Alvarez are excerpted from his introduction to Bertrand Frohman's *Brief Psychotherapy,* part of which I used as a textbook in psychiatry at the L.A.C.C. Let me affirm publicly that I knew Dr. Frohman. He was a gentleman in the finest sense of the term; a real physician with a benevolent inspiring attitude, and a broad intellectual viewpoint. He himself periodically had chiropractic adjustments. Just prior to his death he told me so. I have known other medical psychiatrists who equally have partaken of chiropractic benefits. Some few others condemn irrationally without knowing why they do so.

Over a decade or so ago, Dr. Lawrence Kubie, a prominent figure in the American development of psychoanalysis, wrote a superb book entitled *Practical Aspects of Psychoanalysis.* He was misguided enough in that book to make a couple of very unkind references to the chiropractor. For this irrationality, I wrote him a scathing letter of denunciation. At least he was honest enough, in part, to recognize what he had perpetrated. In his reply to my letter, he said: "I have read it with interest, and, I must say, with profound respect for the fairness with which you treat me after my somewhat flippant crack at your own field. Your letter also challenges me to learn more about a subject in which I must confess medicine"—that is a therapy with no thinking at all," says Alvarez, who then recovers sufficiently of his own medical prejudice to add, "and I am told that in a certain large city the man who does it with the greatest completeness is a chiropractor." Has not Alvarez ever visited some of the large medical machine-shops which peddle prepaid medical insurance schemes? They make any chiropractic advertising house look like child's play. But it seems impossible to the medically-minded practitioner that a chiropractor should dare to compete with a medical man at his own decerebrate game!

Perhaps here attention should be called to the recent scandal in California. Some two hundred physicians have been detected in skull-duggery, swindling a large medical insurance group out of about a million dollars. It is the conventional measurement of medical practice that Moloney wants the chiropractor to emulate? That the county medical association wishes to press charges for the conviction of these physicians has absolutely nothing to do with the issue at all. Is the chiropractor incapable of this? Not at all. I see no difference between them, group for group. People are people, and that is all there is to it. I tremble, however, to think of what the press would have published if these were chiropractors, not medical men involved in the scandal. Moloney, however, like a typically neurotic patient, prefers to gloss over the not-uncommon occurrence he does not wish to see. He needs a scapegoat upon which all of man's sins can be heaped—to be cast out into the wilderness to die a tragic, lonely death. And this, remember, is a psychiatrist speaking!

Heaven only knows I have denounced the average chiropractor who does indeed practice a decerebrate therapy. I have been vociferous in my protestations over current practice. In fact, I have travelled the length and breadth of this state, and seems to have lost none of its power, however; thus the indiscriminate usage. Scientific? Nonsense—this is pure magic.

"Yet he thrives," complains Moloney. "He thrives because he fills a specific emotional need. He completes a gestalt of a precise and inexorably fixed unconscious fantasy." This is the idiocy of neurotic thinking in all its stark nakedness. He cannot realize what is so obviously factual, and which many an other psychiatrist has called attention to, that everything he has said above is equally and even more true of the medical man. The success of the medical doctor is not due entirely to his scientific training, nor to his specific ministrations to the sick. It is because people from the time they were babies, have been taught to regard him as a "medicine man." He is a magician possessed of omniscience and magical powers. Because he waves the wand, uses the magic needle, draws forth the life blood, administers the mystical pills and the alchemical potion, he fills the most deep-seated needs of great numbers of people. His word is like an exorcism or a benediction. His visit in white to the sickroom is comparable to the banishment of the demons of the night. Dr. Howe in *Motives and Mechanisms of the Mind*, calls attention to this phenomenon, and in several of his writings Carl Jung debunks the whole attitude. Does not Moloney know this? If not, then, colloquially, he should have his head examined. He demonstrates his own utter futility as a psychiatrist.

By conventional psychiatric standards, the average medical man is a dope. Let us make no bones about this. In one sense, this is why psychiatry has never "caught on" in modern medicine. There are a mere handful of psychiatrists when you consider the vast numbers of medical pill-rollers, muscle-stabbers with needles, and belly-openers. The psychiatrist, by and large, has utter contempt for most of his tomfoolery. Dr. Alvarez of the Mayo Clinic calls this sort of thing "decerebrate is threatened by the adult." It would appear that Moloney was threatened by his father. Not only did he construct reaction formations to ward off anxiety about his early feelings toward his father. More especially with his father's medical irrationality and prejudice.

"The chiropractor and his ilk cannot be ignored." So runs the prejudicial attitude of an otherwise enlightened man, who, despite all appearances to the contrary, is chained like Prometheus to the rock where his father-vulture can peck at his vitals. "Vituperation and legislation will not dislodge him. He insinuates the pattern of the American fabric. Judged by the accepted standards of physics, his caprices are irrational." Moloney would be well-advised to return to school for a course in physical medicine where he will find many justifications for the chiropractic hypothesis. Moreover, Dr. Ray Lyman Wilbur of Stanford University, wrote that "medicine based on pills and potions is becoming obsolete. The new physiology, with the help of physics, has taught us many ways to deal with the human body that only were dreamed of a decade ago, but comparatively successfully pursued by those of the irregular schools." Study that one, Moloney!

"The chiropractor is unscientific according to the conventional measurement of medical practice." This no doubt is why medicine has stolen Physical Medicine! In addition, I need only to call attention to numbers of articles that have appeared on and off in both professional and lay journals. Some of them bore the caption "Is penicillin losing its power?" It is, so these articles, infer, because all too many physicians use it indiscriminately. They do not take time out to diagnose accurately the condition the patient has brought them. Penicillin is employed as a panacea, the magical remedy, as were the sulfa drugs in the preceding decade, which will cure all ills. The quest for the dollar from his nervous system. Psychoanalysis and all forms of psychotherapy actually have, as their fundamental intent, the conscious extirpation of these unconscious habit-patterns that parents have fostered, so as to enable the individual to make ego-choices, conscious and deliberate determinations of how he will think, feel, and act. For this reason, then, one is all the more surprised when a psychiatrist behaves in such a way as to indicate that he is an unwitting stooge for his parental beliefs. It was just this attitude that his own psychoanalytical training was intended to eliminate.

Moloney's father was a doctor. Forty or fifty years ago, the average medical doctor was irrevocably committed to a condemnation of manipulation, adjustment, and physio-therapy. Their national association had declared vicious war on the chiropractor who was conceived of as a dupe and a dope. The fact that today manipulation and electro-therapy have been sneaked into the backdoor of medicine under the newer label of Physical Medicine has not changed the original situation one iota. The children of those people who once condemned chiropractors have done nothing to indicate that their own emotional maturity on this score has at all improved. Moloney's writing admits that his father's attitudes have had a profound influence upon him, too.

"I do not intend," he writes, "to investigate my father's ideas." Why don't you? It is not enough to state overtly that you have since then learned that in some ways your father was wrong. Your whole set of unreasonable attitudes to the chiropractor indicates that you need urgently to re-examine the basic emotional ground of your thinking. You have written that "it is important to possess knowledge of character development, because character, in this culture, at least, is for the most part a reaction formation against the eruption of anxiety. The child definition, is not an average person. He is supposed to have been psychoanalyzed himself in order to have exposed his own unconscious wish-phantasms. Our good doctor, despite all his brilliance, indicates in his book that he is just such a victim of phylogenetic thinking and phantasy which is utterly appalling. He makes vividly-outlined divisions into Aristotelian blacks and whites, with no space for all sorts of shades of grey in between. He is the victim of wishful, even dishonest thinking—as much as those people whom he deplores and condemns in his book. For him the medical doctor, no matter how temporarily he may be mistaken, is on the side of light. The chiropractor, however right he may accidently be, is on the side of the dark. It is a full-blown dichotomy, as stupid and infantile and neurotic as that perceived by the non-psychiatrically orientated person.

Here is a tragedy which indicates that cultural viewpoints stick, like tar and feathers, to an individual no matter how valiantly he may have striven to free himself from emotional dependencies during infancy. The chiropractor, of course, is just as subject to these as is the medical man. There is utterly no difference. My complaint is that the psychiatrist is usually in an educational area, small that it is, which is totally removed from such stupidities. His entire education—collegiate, social and professional—is dedicated to revealing the emotional complexes with their concomitant mental defenses which arise in the course of ontogenetic development.

Parental viewpoints, which reflect the larger prevailing community and social viewpoints, are pressured upon the growing child, leaving indelible psychic traces which persist disastrously throughout the lifetime. And the individual, no matter how intelligent and enterprising and freedom-loving he may be, rarely is able to eradicate those parental imprints

The need for perfection is firmly planted in the psyche of the growing child by poorly adjusted and fearful parents. They will brook no attitudes, no behavior on the part of the child which in effect expose their own inadequacy and inferiority which is disguised by the psychic armouring of megalomania and perfectionism. As a result of this, the child is subjected to emotional stresses and strains which psychologically cripple him. He is severely traumatized. "It is apparent to all psychiatrists," says Moloney, "that traumata stifle the child and impair his development. Energy is fixated by such traumata. The effect of trauma is difficult to measure...When the infant is traumatized, the infant is confronted with the necessity of creating a phantom authoritarian within his own corporeal confines. This phantom of the parental authority utilizes energy for its creation and maintenance. Energy is bound by the phantom creation. This phantom also requires energy to be available for the purpose of suppressing any individualized effort on the part of the real self. Much energy is denied effective use because the real self must utilize considerable quantities of energy in order to neutralize the restriction of the phantom...This results in a vicious cycle—a compulsive system that requires more and more energy to be sucked from the reservoirs, rendering the personality ever weaker."

When the personality is thus rendered weak, inefficient, and incapable of dealing with its every-day problems, it resorts to phantasy as a means of dealing with those problems. It generally resorts to the creation of a gigantic dichotomy, similar to the earliest theological formulations—good and evil. This inner phantasy is projected indiscriminately on to all and sundry—some people and things are perceived as wholly good and others as wholly bad. It is a common semantic device which the average person is hardly aware of. But the psychiatrist, by the many problems of emotionally disturbed people. I strongly recommend the book to all members of the profession who are struggling to sharpen their vision into similar problems. He has one chapter on "Today's Tomorrow" which enunciates several significant ideas. They are ideas which every individual, regardless of race, creed, or profession would do well to study critically, with a view to incorporation into his own intellectual armamentarium. Our politicians, especially at this time, with a national election ensuing, and with the world today being the powder-keg that it is, should be forced to become familiar with some of these concepts. For example: "Perfectionism is, in reality, a megalomania. It is a megalomania intended to protect the individual from a destructive morality. Megalomania is a surface manifestation, an over-compensation for a feeling of greater inner weakness. Megalomania, born out of weakness, will countenance no weakness in others. The permission of different ideologies subsumes the weakening of the whole structure through the operation of separate cliques...To make every external thing orderly and authorized is the surface aim of such omnipotence. If submissiveness cannot be achieved, then the power is not all-powerful. Unveiled, the feared inner weakness erupts and gives away the pretense."

We see evidences of this in our own profession. Some leaders would have us conform to a single set of ideas, with a single set of professional practices which are perfect in their eyes. Those who do not conform are subjected to abuse, almost libel. Of course, this is not exclusive to us. It is found everywhere. It is so found because, in reality, this is the cultural cornerstone of the authoritarian rule of the family. It is from this familial attitude that there emerge the greatest compulsive drives of so many people—and, in which is to be found the mass etiological factor of the ever-increasing quantity of neurotic manifestations in our patients.

# *CRY HAVOC*
By Israel Regardie
New Falcon Publications, First Edition 2017

Dr. James Clark Moloney is a brilliant psychiatrist. He appears to be gifted with penetrating insight into several emotional problems which the psychiatrist is called upon to deal with. He has written a number of provocative articles, about inter-personal relationships and their dynamic implications, for the popular journals. Some years ago, one of the news-week magazines according him considerable fame about his observations of the psychic structure and relative lack of mental disease amongst the natives of Okinawa where he followed the Marines after their bloody invasion during the last war. *The Magic Cloak* is a book by Dr. Moloney with a subtitle of "A Contribution to the Psychology of Authoritarianism." According to the introduction to the book, Dr. Moloney is a man of multi-interests and activities. He belongs to many societies, medical, psychiatric and psychoanalytical. He also appears to be a member of an anthropological group. At Wayne University he is the assistant professor of Psychiatry. All in all, then, our doctor is a very important person in the psychiatric world. By all normal standards, he should be extraordinarily well-informed.

And he is. The book mentioned above is a powerful piece of writing. It comprises a number of scintillating essays that are not only well written, but indicate very powerful insights into symptoms include the rapid pulse and pounding heart, blushing and excessive sweating of hands and feet, fast but shallow respiration, spasm of the whole digestive tract, and a multitude of sexual difficulties as well. As the muscular attitudes which sustain and maintain these fears are attacked and broken down, the patient may often be seized by an overwhelming fear. This has to be witnessed or experienced to be believed and understood. Only the doctor's sympathy and warmth in a supporting role are of avail here to withstand these mighty onslaughts of panic. The patient does not at first realize them to be the emergence of those awful fears and apprehensions which plagued him as a child. Plagued him so foully that they had to be repressed.

Is it any wonder then that given the much needed opportunity to discharge these and similar emotions, the patient yells, screams, shouts and cries? They may be annoying for the waiting patient to hear; but the patient undergoing such therapy adopts an altogether different attitude. He soon becomes grateful for the chance to express his feelings so vigorously, and without criticism. These are the active devices which he is encouraged and even persuaded to employ on his journey back to full, natural and healthy organismic function. And these are the expressions which spell the end to his neurosis.

inferences, feel emotions, and remember hitherto forgotten painful events more clearly than he could before. In other words, his whole personality function is enhanced. From this integration, his own capacity for personal pleasure, enjoyments and happiness is immeasurably improved.

As these feelings arise, it seems only natural that patients may wish to cry. In this they are encouraged, prodded and aided to sob without inhibition. Crying—not merely with the face and from the eyes, but a sobbing that issues from deep down in the vitals—breaks up residual muscular attitudes that were part of the neurosis. Some patients come to realize that muscular tensions were once necessitously developed to prevent the unwanted occurrence of crying or the emergence of anger. And it was by repression with the assistance of muscular tension that emotional fixation or retardation, which is neurosis, once developed.

In some neurotic conditions, crying is about the only emotional expression which will release and discharge the disturbing symptom. Curiously enough, we find patients who need most to cry are those who are most incapable of crying. No matter how ardently their misery, depression and unhappiness might make them wish to cry, they suffer from an inner emptiness and hardiness which prevents tears. All the skill and sympathy and experience of the doctor have to be directed towards eradicating this tragic block. Sometimes this is more complex than seems at first sight.

Fear and anxiety are yet other emotions which many patients, as children, have learned or have been forced to block off in rigid muscular attitudes. The set jaw, furrowed eyebrows and forehead, tight belly, and tense thigh adductors—all these give eloquent testimony to the chronic emotional strain such harnessed patients have been subjected to. And this, altogether apart form transient attacks of pain and anxiety, with a variety of visceral dysfunctions, which sometimes have made them doubt their own sanity. Such functional relaxation occurs and with it a discharge of the emotions which originally produced the neurotic manifestations, the need for the disturbing symptom disappears. With the need gone, the symptom vanishes. The muscular attitudes have changed because a physical relaxation has developed. In the process of expressing feelings and emotions which he has not dared to recognize or experience for two or three decades, the patient's entire character structure undergoes a profound metamorphosis. The organism can then make its own inherent progressions to emotional maturity.

The orthodox notion insists that neurotic compulsions are due to repressed hostility. Out of the muscular tensions to the neck, chest, belly and back required to anchor this massive quantity of anger and irritability, visceral disturbances must follow. Relaxation of the somatic areas mentioned must therefore release a great deal of anger, aggression, rage and sheer spitefulness. Emotions such as these can hardly be conceptualized. The abreaction of such depth and magnitude of feeling is difficult if not impossible to achieve through verbalization. Specific action is required.

The noises heard in the outer reception room, then, are shouts and yells made by patients as they pound and pummel the couch or padded wall. With the aid of definite technical devices, a state of relative emotional lability can be induced in which, for a short time, the neurotic control by the superego—the psychic censor of thoughts and feelings, the cortical inhibitor of motor activity, the overdeveloped conscience of the neurotic patient—is overridden. The long concealed aggressions can be discharged with some ease and some fullness.

The effect on the patient of such abreaction is extensive. Much inner tension is removed which, by autonomic pathways, reduces visceral and neuromuscular rigidity. Relaxation is the outcome. But this is not all. Psychologically, the patient is able to function more freely. He can conceptualize, verbalize, express judgements and phobias, tics—and some hypochondriacal conditions it was almost impossible to achieve by conventional means. At this historical juncture, therapeutic emphasis was shifted from abreaction to aiding the patient to arrive at insight into the etiology and meaning of his neurotic symptoms. This approach at times is successful; at others it fails lamentably. Because of this uncertainty, many of us have diligently searched for other methods.

Many years ago Wilhelm Reich evolved a method which he called vegeto-therapy. It is admirably suited for the treatment of such refractory cases. There are now locally a number of chiropractors who having undergone the requisite therapy and training themselves are using this method. Vegeto-therapy is based on the premise that emotions are not only cortically represented, but that they spring from and operate through the visceral and muscular systems. That, in effect, emotional tension is accompanied by neuromuscular tension. That character attitudes express themselves through and are functionally identical with body and behavior attitudes. That, moreover, mind and body are phases of a unitary living organism. *Psyche* and *soma* are not only words to be hyphenated, but are symbols of a single biological unit.

The conventional psychotherapies attempt to deal with neurotic conflicts and emotional sterility by conceptual methods, by verbalization and clarification of thinking. Vegeto-therapy approaches this problem from the somatic angle. It seeks not merely to relax muscular hypertonus—chiropractic does that also, and quite successfully. This therapy attempts to *discharge* the disturbing emotions which have hampered the patient's ability to alter his behavior to be consistent with his present-day environment. Environment includes parents, wife, children, friends, employment and social situations. When them badly. They complain to the nurse, asking what villainy or outrage I perpetrate on my patients. Of course, they think of rape and murder, neither of which, the nurse assures them, are being committed. These beliefs are of sufficient importance to warrant an intelligent explanation which will be of service both to doctors in the field and to waiting patients.

My present viewpoint has gradually evolved out of experiment with different technical methods which would result in the maximum improvement of the patient. Over the years I have employed non-directive counseling, psychoanalysis, and modified liberal psychotherapies, hypnotism and hypnoanalysis, and carbon dioxide. All are useful to the therapist's armamentarium. Patients with neurological problems or who need electro-convulsive therapy are referred elsewhere. In the treatment of the conventional neurotic syndromes and some of the common psychosomatic maladies, to which my practice is limited, these methods have proven valuable.

A neurosis is an emotionally induced illness. A person who has not quite succeeded in adapting himself to the exigencies of adult life is neurotic. He has retained infantile patterns of response without altogether being aware he has done so. His behavior is characterized by varying degrees of unawareness. This maladaptation produces symptoms in the intellectual, emotional and the visceral areas. But since they are emotionally induced they cannot be argued away by specious intellectual arguments, nor by moral admonitions or exhortations, nor by suggestion or denial. Freud and the early psychoanalysts constantly strove towards abreaction—a discharge of disturbing emotions—as the pivot of the therapy. They believed that given adequate abreaction a "cure" would be imminent. In hysteria and the anxiety states, abreaction was not difficult to achieve. But in a few severe and chronic psychasthenias—obsessions, compulsions,

Its aim may be an increase in feelings of security, of self-confidence, of spontaneity, and self-respect. Its aim may be an increase in maturity."

Can everyone achieve these aims? Not necessarily. We have to be honest ourselves here, recognizing that we have no magical or miracle method which will cure everybody. But this much may be said. Whoever undertakes psychotherapy honestly and sincerely will receive some modicum of assistance. This varies naturally from person to person.

"This is in fact an extremely valuable corrective for anyone who conceives of psychotherapy, or indeed any other therapy in medicine, as having some magical quality of certainty about it. To be able sometimes to cure, more often to relieve, and always to make a helpful relationship with patients, is a sufficiently high goal for any of us:"

## II

In a previously published article, I suggested that discussion with any patient of techniques used in psychotherapy was unnecessary. All he is interested in is recovery. How it is to be done is usually of little concern to him. All methods are useful in some clinical areas. In this connection a problem recently arose which demands an answer. Some possibilities of misunderstanding need to be cleared away.

I share a common reception room with a group of doctors. My office is sound-proofed with cellotex and heavy drapes. Under ordinary circumstances, the sound of conversation or discussion does not leak through into the reception room. As patients wait outside to consult with one of the other doctors, there are times when much to their consternation they hear shouts, screams and unrestrained sobbing. Such sounds, breaking through the ordinarily satisfactory sound-proofing, disturb nutshell: the healed person is not the original person in whom, through the new orientation, the necessity for the symptom, and therefore the symptom itself, has disappeared."

The viewpoint enunciated here implies that a neurotic symptom or attitude grows out of the rich soil of a neurotic or maladjusted character. This neurotic character, as already indicated, has been nurtured in specific ways by earlier child-parent relationship. In a family setting, a vast and extensive set of events and incidents occur which gradually mould the growing character of the child into what we perceive when psychotherapy is later applied for. Therefore psychotherapy seeks not merely the eradication of the symptom. This would be like painting the exterior of a decrepit building in order to hide the fact that cracks and holes have appeared in the wall surface. But where it is possible, it seeks to engineer a basic change in character and attitudes, in the personality structure. Once this underlying character has been rendered strong, mature and realistic, quite naturally the patient will realize he has not further need for the symptom, whatever it may have been, which he had only required as a device in order to cope with his environment. And as soon as he comes to realize that he no longer needs the symptom, because he understands how it came to be developed and what purpose it served, it will disappear. Thus the patient, after a successful psychotherapy, is in effect a completely newly-orientated person capable of vigorous, healthy and outgoing attitudes to life and to people.

What then are the aims of psychotherapy? "Psychotherapy," wrote Dr. Levine, "has a variety of aims, which are overlapping and complementary. Its aim may be the alleviation or cure of symptoms. Its aim may be an increase in life-happiness. Its aim may be an increase in efficiency or productiveness. Its aim may be an improvement in interpersonal relationships.

easily. For when they find they can weep in the presence of the therapist, and he does not seem surprised, disturbed, angry or inclined to reject them for weeping they undergo an enormous maturation.

On the other hand, should he feel like expressing hostility and anger and resentment at those in his present and past environment, this too must be accepted and encouraged as a normal component of his personality. This acceptance eliminates inner criticism, releases the hostility and so facilitates psychological maturation. Much the same is true of all other emotions—pain of any kind, grief concerning loss of loved ones, fear, shame and guilt. Once the patient realizes—not intellectually, but primarily through the direct emotional impact of personal experience—that whatever his emotions are he can be accepted by the therapist, inner security is gradually restored. And on the firm basis of this emotional security, he can resume the personality growth which was interrupted on an earlier level of development.

This is a magical formula. It is similar to the process of adaptation and maturation under other circumstances of life. There is no magical pill, no magical potion. It represents a certain amount of sincere effort on the part of the patient, effort to acquire an honest and adult recognition of the tremendous possibilities inherent within himself. "It happens only too often that a patient expects at the beginning of an analysis that the psychotherapist will, by some magical means, simply rid him of his symptoms without ever touching the rest of the structure of his life, with which he is quite satisfied. The analyst is only too often supposed to be a kind of 'medicine man,' who will make the symptom disappear from outside. The truth is that nobody can be cured until he is prepared to accept the need for a more or less complete re-orientation of his life. To put it in a

Any other kind of discussion about methods or techniques is relatively useless. Actually, all methods are useful and, of course, all techniques work. For example, Dr. Don Morris wrote last year a most illuminating commentary on psychotherapy in these words: "A number of years ago I had the opportunity of observing several people with anxiety reactions who recovered in the hands of a psychotherapist. These patients were free to talk to me and repeatedly made such statements as this: 'I am getting well, but I haven't the slightest idea what his is talking about. I don't know the meaning of the words he uses.' It became clear that healing was taking place in the realm of feelings, and that perhaps we should not take our techniques in the intellectual sense too seriously; that more than one 'technique' will get us to the same goal."

With this, I heartily concur. In fact, I have stressed again and again that intellectualization in the realm of psychotherapy is relatively useless. What is needed above all is to give the patient the much needed opportunity to express his feelings about himself, his environment, and his earlier family situations. If he feels like crying, this should be encouraged. He must be taught that not only do sissies cry, but men can cry too. I like to call the attention of the patient to some of the early classics, in which one of the great Greek heroes is informed that a warrior friend has been killed in battle. Thereupon the hero sits down and weeps freely and openly. None think he is effeminate, and none would dare doubt his valour. In a recent book on the American Revolution, there is a touching account of George Washington's farewell to LaFayette. Washington embraces him—and weeps. None can question Washington's greatness, nor his manliness, yet he wept.

It is good for patients to know this, for then they will feel no anxiety and can accept themselves and their emotions more

"This is the meaning of 'neurotic' in the broad sense: inappropriate ways of thinking, attitudes, moods and behavior which arise from infantile motivations or their derivatives or reactions against them." Dr. Saul implies by this that infantile types of behavior operate in the psychoneuroses, and that all the symptoms are the product of earlier patterns of response.

What then does the psychiatrist do about this? If the patient who presents a mass of psychoneurotic symptoms is, in effect, a person who has not quite succeeded in adapting himself to adult life and has retained some infantile patterns of response, how does the therapist proceed to restore to the patient his integrity on a true adult level? There are many methods of doing this. Sometimes patients ask about the methods employed, but this I think is the exclusive province of the therapist. I doubt the wisdom of discussing at length with the patient the kind of approach or method that is employed.

Above all other things, what is required of the patient is that he learn to communicate his feelings about his problems to the doctor. He is asked to talk, to verbalize his experiences, to discuss what has occurred to him at various periods of his life-history. As the patient talks, first about this, and then that, and later about some other thing, a great deal of the inner tension is discharged. An emotional relaxation develops as the patient, by discussion, become desensitized to his former difficulties. This is expressed extremely well by Dr. Cameron: "To talk out our reaction to a situation is to relive that situation, and the more extensively and intensively it can be talked out, the more completely it is relived. To relive a situation in a supportive setting, e.g., the patient-therapist relationship, is to modify our reaction to it in the sense of freeing that reaction from whatever hostility, anxiety, guilt or embarrassment it may be invested with."

fundamentally normal feelings are rejected, forced into inhibition, and utterly repudiated. The result is that the patient learns, from parental attitudes, that certain feeling responses are not acceptable to them. If he shows them in any way, he will be punished in one form or another. As the years go by, naturally these feelings clamor for expression. Given no normal exit, they force a surreptitious outlet by devious routes, gradually creating what we conveniently call neurotic symptoms. Briefly, these psychoneurotic symptoms are the product of a group of emotional relationships or attitudes to life—attitudes which have been developed by virtue of the much earlier family setting. The family setting is the soil in which grows and develops the personality of the child. "The influence exerted upon the personal structure by the long period of dependency has great significance for psychotherapy, since the way in which the child relates himself to parental figures greatly affects not only the way in which he will relate himself to others, but also the way in which he will relate himself to the therapist during treatment. From these primary relationships may be derived, for instance, a fear of excessively close relationships, or a pattern of relationship in terms of hostility, or a tendency towards excessive dependency..."

In other words whatever were the attitudes the child had to develop within the family circle in the early years of life, so will he continue rigidly to react in later life. He learns a pattern of responses first to the people in his immediate environment, which later become extended to all others. But, generally speaking, whatever those patterns were once, so will they continue to be. Most of the time, flexibility in adjustment is lost in those early years, and a stereotyped pattern of response is employed in many life-situations where it is hardly warranted. This produces tension, fear, and anxiety, and further maladjustments.

part of the patient. My definition presumes that the psychoneurotic patient, in effect, has not been honest with himself—nor with those about him. This dishonesty is certainly not his fault. It is the product of his family background, of his social and domestic training. The fact remains, however, regardless of whose fault it is, that he is dishonest. He has not been able to confront certain sets of his feelings, normal to all of us, that at one time or another in his life created difficulties with other people. As Dr. Harry Stack Sullivan once said, these psychoneurosis is nothing more nor less than a complex series of organismic devices to alleviate anxiety. Anxiety, a first cousin of fear, is one of those emotions which is utterly intolerable to the patient. He will do almost anything to avoid its experience. Whenever anxiety is evoked by any life-situation or interpersonal relationship, past or present, then these adjustment devices come into automatic operation to alleviate the strain and tension. Prolonged, and used again and again, this usage becomes habitual and chronic. Out of this chronic use of such devices, the neurotic symptoms are initiated.

Dr. Leon J. Saul confirms this viewpoint, and at the same time amplifies it still further, in these words:

"The aim of therapy…is to help the patient recognize and appreciate as fully as possible, his true impulses and desires, to free them from the automatic operation of the inhibiting forces and bring them under the purview of conscious realization and judgement, so that rigidity and automaticity of reaction can yield to greater flexibility, conscious choice and the reopening of this hitherto blocked part of the personality to further development."

It is my contention that faulty training is responsible for this inability on the part of the patient to tolerate his feelings and impulses. Parental attitudes have been such that what are ample evidence that, in some way, the individual has failed in his ability to adjust emotionally to his environment, to the events of his everyday life. He usually does not seek help because of this dimly perceived feeling that he has failed to make an adequate adjustment, of which failure he is heartily ashamed. Strain has become added to strain, tension and anxiety piles up, forcing the individual to develop additional behavior mannerisms which, it is blindly hoped, will alleviate the strain and tension. Most of the time, further problems and strains are created by the symptoms, and thus a vicious cycle is formed. Its only effect is to create despair and hopelessness.

It is usually then that the patient seeks advice and guidance from his physician. More often than not, the physician himself has not been suitably orientated, during his college training, to the implications of psychological factors as they relate to disease. Sometimes a well-educated layman is far better informed in this respect than are many physicians. Be that as it may, the doctor attempts to treat his patient by various physical means. Commonly the patient leaves, drifting from one doctor to another, until such time as one of them, recognizing the inherent emotional difficulty, refers the patient to a psychiatrist for adequate psychotherapy.

The patient at this juncture usually asks "What is psychotherapy? And what is this psychiatrist going to do to me? Will he think I'm nuts?" Unless the doctor has either read widely or has been properly orientated in his college training, he is not likely to provide a good, that is, rational answer to this set of inquiries. What I wish to do here is to provide for the interested physician and his patient some answers to these commonly raised questions.

To me, psychotherapy represents nothing else but an attempt to induce some degree of personal self-honesty on the responses, and in those who are maladjusted facilitates the onset of neurotic symptoms.

Quite often employment difficulties are perceived to be the prime expression of a personal maladjustment. Some people appear to find it practically impossible to retain a job for any length of time. Upon one pretext or another they find one job intolerable, shift to another, and then to yet another. At no time do they seem to find the most congenial or satisfying job. They become suspicious, belligerent, and anti-social. Any decent, forthright kind of relationship with employers or with fellow employees becomes wholly impossible, upon one pretext or another. Their entire employment history is one of constant dissatisfaction, frustration and change. On the other hand, there are those who having found one job, appear to lose all initiative and ambition, clinging to it throughout the years, afraid of making a single move to better themselves. Their personal insecurity is so vast and extensive that they seem unable aggressively to seek further opportunities for growth and advancement.

Many of the so-called female diseases come within this category too. The inevitable monthly pains, excessive or inadequate menstrual flow, accumulation of fatty deposits on hips or elsewhere, difficult or undesired sexual relationships, are only a few of the many complex symptom-problems that arise here in connection with some endocrinopathy. All too often these are only the superficial evidences that the emotional life of the individual is highly disturbed. And it is inevitable that nothing allays the physical difficulties until the disturbed emotional life is dealt with and straightened out.

Other typical neurotic problems are shyness, laziness, insomnia, stammering, sexual deviations, alcoholism, the so-called nervous breakdown, delinquency, excessive gambling, criminality, and many another. All these and hosts besides give pathology or somatic disease process. These symptoms include an extraordinarily wide variety of gastric symptoms ranging from occasional bouts of indigestion to cramps, nausea and stomach ulcers. A close second are cardiac symptoms, ranging again from simple palpitations and a so-called nervous heart, to the more serious coronary symptoms and high blood pressure. Headaches with all their variations again are other symptoms. Most authorities today agree that only ten percent of those with headaches suffer from some bona fide physical disease, the other ninety percent are involved in some form of emotional tensions.

Any textbook of psychiatry lists a large array of symptoms, involving many organs, limbs, tissues, and physiological systems. These are almost too numerous to mention. Then there are other symptoms however which are purely psychological. The person who is depressed and pessimistic, who takes a jaundiced view of life, who swings easily from hysterical laughter to equally hysterical weeping. Then there is the patient who despite several first-rate psychic assets—a good family background, good education, good looks and physique, and a well-equipped mind—feels utterly worthless and inadequate. They use all sorts of shabby devices to gain approbation from their friends and families. Nothing however really alleviates their feelings of inferiority.

Many marital problems are in reality related to the psychoneuroses. Difficulties in mutual adjustment on sexual, intellectual and religious levels can be distinctly traced long anterior to the time of marriage. A careful history of one or both of the marriage partners usually indicates a life-history replete with emotional problems of many kinds. Upon marriage, these difficulties are merely carried over into the marriage situation. Marriage merely acts as a catalyst to hasten the emotional

# WHAT IS PSYCHOTHERAPY
By Israel Regardie
New Falcon Publications, First Edition 2017

Every now and again, a physician requests of me as to how he should orientate a patient, who needs counselling, about this need. "What shall I tell this patient without offending him—without confirming him in already formulated view that only crazy people go to see a psychiatrist?"

This is one of today's most blatant misconceptions and unfortunately, it is held not only by the patients who may need psychotherapy most, but by some physicians who should know better. The days have long since vanished when the psychiatrist was cloistered behind the forbidding walls of the insane asylum. To-day, he is an integral part of the community, functioning not merely as an expert on those serious mental diseases known as psychoses, but also as a counsellor, advisor and consultant for untold thousands of people who periodically have become submerged by one emotional problem or another. It is to these people that he ministers, to the ordinary people that both you and I know in every-day life.

What kind of people, then, go to the psychiatrist? There are very many people who do need his services. Rough estimates calculate that in this country there are not merely thousands but several million people who have all kinds of physical and emotional symptoms which are unrelated directly to any physical